The Noahide Guide to
Matthew

The Noahide Guide to Matthew

Alan W. Cecil

Academy of Shem Press
Estero, Florida

Copyright © 5769/2009 by Alan W. Cecil

Academy of Shem Press
21301 S. Tamiami TRL STE 320
Estero, FL 33928

All rights reserved. No part of the publication may be reproduced, stored in a retrieval system or transmitted, in any form, or by any means, electronic, mechanical, recorded, photocopied, or otherwise, without the prior permission of the copyright owner, except by a reviewer who may quote brief passages in a review.

Cover design by Jeremy Hulsey

Cover Illustrations
Front: *St. Matthew* by Caravaggio
Back: *Matthew and the Angel* by Rembrandt

ISBN: 978-0-9779885-1-8

www.academyofshem.com

Printed in the United States of America

*To Layla,
whose long hours of research and hard work made
this manuscript possible…*

Contents

Introduction
9

Translations of the Text
17

The Greek Manuscripts
22

The Primary Sources
31

Matthew
41

Introduction

Handbooks of NT [New Testament] textual criticism appear at the rate of only one or two in each generation, so that the appearance of a new introduction to the discipline attracts the attention of all in the field, particularly if it is one written by two of the world's most influential NT textual critics. Kurt and Barbara Aland's The Text of the New Testament appeared in German in 1982 and in English in 1987. The last standard work of this kind, by Bruce M. Metzger, was published in 1964, with an abiding (though now dated) second edition of 1968.[1]

—Eldon Jay Epp

As most Christians are well aware, the original church in Jerusalem led by James, Peter, and John was little more than a Jewish sect. What is less known is that these Torah-observant Jews were not teaching the later-developed and now-familiar theology of the church, but a teaching of Judaism which dealt with non-Jews, the Seven Laws of Noah.[2] This is why the need for a commentary and book of New Testament criticism from the Noahide perspective—the perspective of the Torah-observant non-Jew—is long overdue. To date, the overwhelming majority of commentaries and textual criticisms on the New Testament have been written from a Christian theological or cultural viewpoint, and during the last half of the twentieth century, most New Testament "textual criticism" has focused on the wealth of ancient Greek manuscripts that have surfaced over the past century and a half and how the corruptions in the different manuscripts obfuscate the true meaning of the "original text." Of course, if the original church was indeed a Jewish sect that taught within the paradigm of Torah Law, arguments about the "original text," to say nothing of Christian theology, would be rendered moot.

---

[1] Eldon Jay Epp, *New Testament Textual Criticism Past, Present, and Future: Reflections on the Alands' "Text of the New Testament" The Harvard Theological Review*, Vol. 82, No. 2, (Apr., 1989), 214.

[2] The Noahide Law, or the Seven Laws of Noah, is the ancient moral and legal code taught by the rabbis before, during, and after the time of Jesus. According to Judaism, a non-Jew is not under the entire Torah (the five books of Moses), but only has to refrain from idolatry, blasphemy, murder, theft, illicit sex, eating the limb of a living animal, and to establish courts of justice.

The evidence for the original church teaching the Noahide Law is found in the New Testament book of Acts, the only book we have about the early decades of the church. Chapter 15 of Acts documents a pivotal event in Christian history: the inclusion of gentiles into the nascent Jerusalem church.[3] This matter was a major issue and the crux of a debate between the Hellenists, led by Paul of Tarsus, and the leaders of the Jewish church, led by James, the brother of Jesus, and the original Jewish apostles. James had not been one of the apostles when Jesus was alive; it was only after Jesus's death that he became the leader of the Jerusalem church, no doubt because as the brother of Jesus and of Davidic descent, James was next in line for the throne. This alone shows that the early church was indeed a political movement, and it certainly fits in with the apostle's question in Acts 1:6, "When they therefore were come together, they asked of him, saying, lord, wilt thou at this time restore again the kingdom to Israel?" It was, however, the battle for the interpretations of Jesus's teachings that was the true battle for the soul of Christianity, and this was the struggle that flows as an undercurrent throughout the book of Acts, particularly after Paul comes into the picture.

When the gentiles started to join the ranks of the Jewish Christians, James and the other Jewish leaders held a meeting in Jerusalem to settle this question: What do we do with the gentiles? Many of the Jewish leaders thought the gentiles should be circumcised, become full Jewish proselytes, and keep the Jewish law, whereas others thought that this was too great a burden to place upon the non-Jewish followers of the sect. After debate on the issue, James, the brother of Jesus and leader of the Jerusalem church, made his decision. Rather than being circumcised and having to keep the Jewish law, gentiles who wanted to join the Jewish sect were only to abstain from idolatry, illicit sex, and blood, and, as given in some of the earliest recorded witnesses of Acts 15:20, to obey the prohibition of "what is hateful to yourself, do not do to another."

---

[3] "This [Apostolic Council] forms the watershed of Acts, what precedes leading up to the formal recognition of Gentile Christianity and what follows describing its future progress." W. K. Lowther Clarke, *Concise Bible Commentary*. (London: SPCK, 1952), 810.

To most Christians, this would seem to be a trivial matter, the earliest texts of Acts having been changed from the negative form of the Golden Rule to the more familiar "and things strangled." This is, however, far from being a minor alteration, for it ties James's ruling in with a teaching of Jewish law, a part of the Jewish law that is specifically given to gentiles and known as the Seven Laws of Noah, or the Noahide Law.[4] In the Talmud (*Shabbat* 31a) there is a famous story about a Noahide who asks the renowned Rabbi Hillel[5] to teach him the Torah while standing on one foot, that is to say, quickly. Rabbi Hillel responds, "What is hateful to yourself, do not do to another. The rest is commentary: go study it." This is the essence of the Noahide Code in a nutshell, and the pithy quote of "what is hateful to yourself, do not do to another" in Acts is clearly a reference to Hillel's answer to the Noahide.[6] To cover all bases, James also included the three absolute prohibitions of idolatry, adultery, and murder. According to Jewish law, the 613 *mitzvot*, or commandments, found in the Torah of Moses can be transgressed to preserve one's life. The exceptions, which a Jew cannot violate even to preserve his own life, are idolatry, adultery, and murder.[7] These three prohibitions correspond to the three prohibitions mentioned (along with Hillel's dictum) by James in Acts 15:20: pollutions of idols (idolatry), fornication (adultery), and blood (murder). According to this ruling, the gentiles were to observe the Noahide Law but not to become full proselytes to Judaism. More importantly, the church was still under the auspices of Jewish law. The later Christian theological concepts of having to believe in Jesus, the trinity, and being "saved by grace" are not

---

[4] The Noahide Law is a moral and legal code made up of seven laws: the prohibition of idolatry, blasphemy, murder, illicit sex, theft, unnecessarily harming animals (literally, "not to eat the limb of a living animal"), and the establishment of courts of justice (*Sanhedrin* 56a–60a). These represent the areas of Jewish law in which a non-Jew can be held liable in a *beis din*, or Jewish (or Noahide) court of law.

[5] Rabbi Hillel was one of the great sages of the late Second Temple era. He died in the first decade of the Common Era.

[6] "[I]n its description of the Jerusalem conference, Acts 15 leaves the clear impression that Paul agreed to instruct Gentile converts to keep the Noahide Commandments. In fact, Acts stresses this point by a double recitation of these commandments in Acts 15:20 and 15:29." Dixon Slingerland, *"The Jews" in the Pauline Portion of Acts. Journal of the American Academy of Religion*, Vol. 54, No. 2, (Summer, 1986), 305.

[7] This does not include killing in self-defense when there is no other option to stop an attacker.

mentioned. Later Christian theologians, faced with the problem of the early church's being "too Jewish," tried to solve the problem by explaining that the early apostles simply did not understand the teachings of Jesus in a theological sense (as evidenced, for example, by their question about the restoration of the kingdom of Israel in Acts 1:6). It was only many decades later that theologians more deeply considered the events depicted in the Gospels and came to full realization of the true "knowledge" of the teachings of Jesus. The problem with this viewpoint, of course, is that it makes the eyewitnesses of the life and teaching of Jesus less relevant to Christianity than those who came later. Jesus's own disciples, not to mention his own siblings, were considered not to have understood his theology as well as those, like Paul of Tarsus, who had never known Jesus or actually heard him teach.

If the early Jerusalem church taught the Noahide Code to the non-Jews who were joining their movement, how and why did this church morph into the decisively non-Jewish church? Christian explanations have been less than credible. The original (Jewish) church had no intention of being "emancipated" from the law, and they certainly did not believe that it had been "suspended by the Christian redeemer," a point that is clarified by the New Testament itself. In chapter 21 of Acts, after Paul has returned from his third missionary tour, he is called on the carpet for the second time by James and the other leaders of the church, who received disturbing news about many of his teachings. They have heard, for example, that Paul has been teaching that the law has been "suspended by the Christian redeemer" and that Jewish Christians are now "emancipated" from it. James tells Paul that the Jerusalem church not only keeps the Torah, but that they are all "zealous for the law" (Acts 21:20). In order to prove that these rumors are false and to show that Paul himself keeps the *mitzvot* of the Torah, James and the other elders order Paul to go to the Temple with four other men and pay their expenses (for the sacrifices). They order Paul himself to offer a sacrifice to show that he keeps the Torah. They also tell him that there will not be any more nonsense about the law being "suspended by the Christian redeemer." Abandoning the usual braggadocio we see in his epistles, Paul meekly submits to James and the elders of the church, and "then Paul took the men, and the next day purifying himself with them entered into the temple, to signify the accomplishment of the days of purification, until that an offering should be offered for every one of them" (Acts 21:26).

Hillel's teaching, "what is hateful to yourself, do not do to another" (Acts 15:20 and 15:29), is also found in the early Western texts of the New Testament.[8] The Western text was the version used by nearly all of the church fathers in the second and early third centuries.[9] We know that the original version of Acts 15:20 contained Hillel's dictum, for the earliest quotation we have of Acts 15:20 comes from the second-century church father, Irenaeus, in *Against Heresies*, book iii.12:14, which quotes Hillel's maxim instead of the spurious "and things strangled." If this is the original passage—and there certainly is no reason to think otherwise—then James and the other leaders of the Jerusalem church were observant Jews "zealous for the law."[10] This would have grave implications for Christianity, not only for those critics who complain that the Seven Laws of Noah are not found in scripture, but also for Christian theology *per se*. If the church deliberately altered the texts of the New Testament and changed the fundamental teachings of the leaders of the Jerusalem church, who were the original apostles of Jesus, it would affect the very authority of the church itself and its claims to "apostolic succession."

Chapter 21 of Acts is the last we hear of the church of the original apostles. The rest of the history of the church is the history of Paul and his Hellenistic followers. In fact, from the Jerusalem council mentioned in Acts 15 to the account of the brief but enlightening submission to the Jewish Church in Jerusalem, the entire second half of Acts deals with Paul and the Hellenistic

---

[8] "A passage which presents great difficulties [Acts 15:20]. The Western text omits 'and from what is strangled' and, in some MSS., adds 'and whatsoever they do not wish to be done to themselves not to do to others'. It therefore turns the decree into a moral law…[s]ome light is thrown on it by the so-called 'Noachian commands', said by the Rabbis to be binding on all men." Clarke, *Concise Bible Commentary*, 811.

[9] "Of course, the text which some scholars would still call 'Western', the text of Justin Martyr, Marcion, Tatian and Tertullian, is much older than and very different from the 'normal', Alexandrian text postulated by the Alands." Gilles Quispel, *The Text of the New Testament by K. Aland ; B. Aland. Vigiliae Christianae*, Vol. 43, No. 4, Dec., 1989. 411.

[10] Acts 21:20.

churches that he founded during his missionary journeys. At the close of Acts, sometime in the early sixth decade of the first century of the Common Era, a great darkness descends on the history of the church, a darkness that will last for decades. When the mists first start to clear, nearly a hundred years later, we see an astonishing change in the church. Gone is the Jewish leadership. Gone are the original Jewish teachings of the Noahide Laws. Gone is the focus on the Torah. The Church has morphed into something quite different. These differences are reflected in a body of writings that would alter the history of the Western world.

These major issues have not been sufficiently dealt with by modern Christian commentators such as Metzger and Aland:
- The primacy of the Western text.
- The theological interpretation of a New Testament devoid of rabbinic commentary.
- The substitution of a Hellenistic instead of a Jewish context.
- The role that the creation and development of the New Testament played in the power struggle between early Christian/Gnostic sects.

To a Christian, interpreting the New Testament from a nontheological perspective would seem absurd, if not blasphemous. Yet since its earliest days, Christianity has interpreted the *Tanach* from a theological viewpoint and has never allowed the New Testament to be interpreted from a Jewish viewpoint. The idea of interpreting a text about a Jewish rabbi and a Jewish movement in ancient Israel using a Noahidic perspective and rabbinic commentary has always terrified the church, which has too many skeletons in its theological closet. As hard as Christian theologians have tried to cover up the evidence, they knew that Judaism holds the key to unlock their darkest secrets.

Translations of the Text

We start with the least problematic, though still disturbing issue concerning the New Testament: the translation of the Greek text into English. For nearly three hundred years, the King James, or Authorized Version, written in poetic but archaic Shakespearean English, was the undisputed English translation, and it is still popular even today, despite the fact that there are many different translations. Some, such as *The Living Bible*, a translation that was popular in the early 1970s, are paraphrased versions. Modern translations include the New International Version and the New American Standard Version. Because few Christians can read the original Greek texts, they are forced to trust the translators. But the way the Greek text of the New Testament is translated often has an impact on theology. To see how this works, let us compare some English translations. We can start with Matthew 5:17, a saying of Jesus that is also given in the Talmud: "I come not to destroy the Law of Moses, nor to add to the Law of Moses" (*Shabbat* 116b). The meaning here is clear: Jesus did not come to alter the Torah in any way.

But The Christian interpretation, which is based on the translation as well as the Greek texts, is different. Starting with the King James Version, which was published in 1611 and has undergone several revisions, the text of Matthew 5:17 is as follows:

> *Think not that I am come to destroy the law, or the prophets: I am not come to destroy, but to fulfil.*

Here the translation shows the differences between the Talmudic Aramaic and the New Testament Greek. In the Christian version, Jesus does not say he is not to "add" to the law, but to "fulfil" [*sic*.], or perform, it. It has more or less the same meaning as the Talmudic version: Jesus did not come to change the law.

Here is another translation, taken from the popular New International Version:

> *Do not think that I have come to abolish the Law or the Prophets; I have not come to abolish them but to fulfill them.*

As we can see, although the wording is slightly different, the meaning is more or less the same as the King James Version.

There are other translations that are popular with the public. These translations are more highly paraphrased. This next example is from the New Living Bible, a late twentieth-century translation:

> *Don't misunderstand why I have come. I did not come to abolish the law of Moses or the writings of the prophets. No, I came to accomplish their purpose.*

Another translation, the New Life Version, is even more paraphrased:

> *Do not think that I have come to do away with the Law of Moses or the writings of the early preachers. I have not come to do away with them but to complete them.*

Notice that this version describes the Hebrew prophets as "early preachers," giving a Christian twist to the text, and is more explicit in giving a theological interpretation to "completing" the law.

Many Christians understand that these are merely translations and that the interpretation of the Greek text depends on the skill and theology of the interpreter. What most Christians do not realize is that the ancient Greek texts used to translate the English New Testament are themselves as different as the examples given above. Here is an example from the King James Version of Matthew 24:36:

> *But of that day and hour knoweth no man, no, not the angels of heaven, but my Father only.*

This verse comes from chapter 24, in which Jesus discusses future events, and that he states that the hour of redemption is known to neither man nor the angels, but only to God. Now, compare this verse with other translations:

> *No one knows about that day or hour, not even the angels in heaven, <u>nor the Son</u>, but only the Father* (NIV).

> *But of that day and hour no one knows, not even the angels of heaven, <u>nor the Son</u>, but the Father alone* (New American Standard Bible).

> *But no one knows the day or the hour. No! Not even the angels in heaven know. <u>The Son does not know</u>. Only the Father knows* (New Life Version).
>
> *However, no one knows the day or hour when these things will happen, not even the angels in heaven <u>or the Son himself</u>. Only the Father knows* (New Living Translation).

These other verses are basically the same, with one important difference: the underlined words *nor the son* are not found in the King James Version. This is an important theological omission, for it implies that even Jesus himself does not know the exact hour of the events he had been speaking of to the apostles. The phrase "nor the son" is found in the early Greek texts, but in later texts it has been deliberately removed.

Here is another verse, one that is even more theologically important, from the Sermon on the Mount, Matthew 6:13. This is the final verse of the Lord's Prayer, which is arguably the most important prayer in Christianity. This is the King James Version:

> *And lead us not into temptation, but deliver us from evil: For thine is the kingdom, and the power, and the glory, for ever. Amen.*

Another translation from the Amplified Bible that has slightly different wording says the same thing:

> *And lead (bring) us not into temptation, but deliver us from the evil one. For Yours is the kingdom and the power and the glory forever. Amen.*

But compare these two with two other modern translations:

> *And lead us not into temptation, but deliver us from the evil one* (NIV).
>
> *And do not bring us to the time of trial, but rescue us from the evil one* (New Revised Standard Version).

Both of these translations leave out the words *For thine is the kingdom, and the power, and the glory, for ever. Amen.* Both an entire sentence and the word *Amen* are missing. Why would the translators leave out an entire sentence in the most famous prayer in the New Testament, a prayer that Jesus transmitted to his disciples? If this was a prayer that Jesus himself taught, and since Christians consider Jesus to be God incarnate, is this not tantamount to editing God's own words?

Let us look at two more examples. The first is Matthew 18:11.

For the Son of man is come to save that which was lost (KJV).

For the Son of Man has come to save that which was lost (New American Standard Bible).

For the Son of Man has come to save that which was lost (New Life Version).

This is another famous saying of Jesus, and the meaning of all three verses is identical. In fact, the New American Standard Bible and the New Life versions are exactly the same. And here is a version that is not only more paraphrased, but also has a theological comment included:

For the Son of man came to save [from the penalty of eternal death] that which was lost (Amplified Bible).

Even with the theological inclusion, the meaning is more or less the same as the other examples of Matthew 18:11. If we compare these translations to other modern translations, such as the New International Version or the New Revised Standard Version, we notice that this verse does not exist in these two translations. The text of Matthew chapter 18 has a verse 10 and a verse 12, but no verse 11. An entire verse—one of Jesus's most famous sayings—is not found in the text of early Greek manuscripts.

Our last example is Matthew 23:14:

Woe unto you, scribes and Pharisees, hypocrites! for ye devour widows' houses, and for a pretence make long prayer: therefore ye shall receive the greater damnation (KJV).

Woe to you, scribes and Pharisees, pretenders (hypocrites)! For you swallow up widows' houses and for a pretense to cover it up make long prayers; therefore you will receive the greater condemnation and the heavier sentence (Amplified Bible).

It is bad for you, teachers of the Law and proud religious law-keepers, you who pretend to be someone you are not! (You take houses from poor women whose husbands have died. Then you try to cover it up by making long prayers. You will be punished all the more because of this.) (New Life Version).

In the New International Version, the Revised Standard Version, and the New Revised Standard Version, this verse, like Matthew 18:11, does not exist. It has been left out, deleted, excised. There are many examples like this, not just in the Gospel of Matthew, but throughout the New Testament. Most Christians are unaware of these differences, and many either do not understand why the translators would leave out important verses or why they would insert phrases that would cause theological problems such as the "nor the son" phrase in 24:36.

What needs to be pointed out is that these differences have nothing to do with the translation. They represent *differences in the Greek texts themselves*. If differences in translations from the Greek have an impact on how we read the New Testament, think of the implications of using different Greek texts, texts that themselves have different wording.

The Greek Manuscripts

There is strong internal testimony that the Gospels were written at an early date...this evidence leads us to believe that the first three Gospels were all composed within 30 years from the time these events occurred.

—Josh McDowell[11]

The standard scholarly dating, even in very liberal circles, is Mark in the 70s, Matthew and Luke in the 80s, John in the 90s. But listen: that's still within the lifetimes of various eyewitnesses of the life of Jesus.

—Lee Strobel[12]

The interval then between the dates of original composition and the earliest extant evidence becomes so small as to be in fact negligible, and the last foundation for any doubt that the [New Testament] Scriptures have come down to us substantially as they were written has now been removed.

—Sir Frederic Kenyon[13]

In his popular book, *The Case for Christ*, Lee Strobel begins with several chapters that discuss the importance of "eyewitness testimony" and the lessons he learned as a journalist. Applying these principles to the Greek New Testament, he says that the writers of the gospels were actual eyewitnesses to Jesus's teaching. He mentions Papias,[14] who was quoted in the fourth century by Eusebius, the Father of Church Propaganda, as saying that Mark had written down the sayings of Peter and that Matthew had written a gospel in Hebrew. Strobel also tells us that Irenaeus claims that

---

[11] Josh McDowell and Don Stewart, *Answers to Tough Questions,* Wheaton, Illinois: Living Books, 1980, 25.

[12] Lee Strobel, *The Case for Christ,* Grand Rapids: Zondervan, 1998, 33.

[13] Sir Frederic Kenyon, *The Bible and Archaeology,* New York: Harper and Row, 1940, 288–89.

[14] The Church's argument of an early date for Mark's gospel rests on the fourth century works of Eusebius, who looked at historical truth as merely a matter of convenience. His only proof was quoting a source known to us as *Papias the Stupid* ("For he [Papias] appears to have been of very limited understanding, as one can see from his discourses.") Eusebius, *Church History*, book iii., ch. 39.

the apostles wrote the Gospels.[15] What Strobel fails to mention is that there is not a single "eyewitness testimony" to the written Gospels by any church father before the mid-second century (about 150 CE), even though the early church fathers often speak of Paul's writings as well as the written *Tanach*. For over a hundred years after Jesus's death, there was no mention of any gospel texts. If Jesus's teachings were transmitted orally and written down in the mid-second century, this would be a serious blow to Christian claims that the apostles and their immediate followers (such as Mark and Luke) wrote the Gospels. In fact, it would cast doubt on the teaching that all twenty-seven books of the New Testament were penned in the first century, beginning with Paul's first epistles around the year 49 CE, and ending with John writing his Apocalypse fifty years later

In the mid-nineteenth century, scholars and archeologists started finding ancient texts of the Greek New Testament stashed away in monasteries and buried in desert trash heaps. These texts were far older than the medieval texts used by the translators of the 1611 Authorized (King James) Version of the New Testament. Two of the most spectacular finds, the Codex Sinaiticus (which had the complete New Testament) and Codex Vaticanus (which was almost complete, though it broke off in the middle of the book of Hebrews), were thought to have been two of the fifty texts of the Bible that Constantine requested Eusebius to produce in the early fourth century. Also discovered were ancient papyrus fragments of the New Testament, some of which were dated going back to the second century CE.

Excited at first, the scholars soon realized there was a problem. These ancient but newly-discovered Greek texts of the New Testament were substantially different from the Byzantine text the church had used for so many centuries. Many of the missionary's favorite "proof-texts," such as 1 John 5:7–8 and Acts 8:37, were not in any of the ancient texts. In fact, many of the favorite verses and stories used by the missionaries seemed to be missing. These are verses about Jesus's divinity, the virgin birth, and Jesus's miracles,

---

[15] This is the same Irenaeus who quoted Acts 20:15 as *what is hateful to yourself, do not do to another*.

theologically important verses that had been major weapons in the missionary's arsenal but were not found in these ancient documents. As scholars went back and read over the writings of the early church fathers, they noticed that many of these "proof texts" were absent from the writings of the early church as well. Differences in the five thousand Greek manuscripts of the Greek New Testament texts number into the hundreds of thousands and are too numerous to be explained away by any logical argument. Yet the missionaries continued to smile and respond like the actor David Leisure (the man who played the incorrigible liar "Joe Isuzu" in those humorous Isuzu car commercials of the late 1980s): *There is nothing wrong with the Greek texts. You have my word on it!*

With the legalization of Christianity at the beginning of the fourth century, the church in Rome began the slow processes of organization, politicalization, and bureaucratization. There were changes in how the stories and teachings of Jesus were written, collected, and transmitted. One of the first steps the church took was the canonization of the New Testament. There were major disagreements as to which books were considered apostolic; some favored books such as the Epistle of Barnabas and the Shepherd of Hermes, and many thought books such as Second Peter and Revelation were obvious forgeries. In 367 CE, Athanasius, the bishop of Alexandria, wrote a festal letter which listed—for the very first time—the twenty-seven books of the New Testament that we recognize today. Within a few decades, this list was agreed on, and the canon was closed.

Another important step was the standardization of the text of the New Testament. In addition to the problem with the many different gospels and epistles, there were also many different versions of the books of Matthew, Mark, Luke, John, Acts, Paul's epistles, and so on. The original, earliest, and most widespread text, the Western text, was edited sometime in the late third century into a smoother and more readable Greek text, which we now call the Byzantine text. Another text that was developed around the same time was the Alexandrian text. Although it was quite popular in Egypt, this text was later discarded in favor of the Byzantine text. Keep in mind that these three texts, the Western, the Alexandrian, and the Byzantine, were fundamentally different from one another in hundreds (if not thousands) of ways. Differences between the Western text of Acts and the Alexandrian text of Acts are astonishing; there is nearly ten percent more material in the Western text. And if that was not confusing enough, near the beginning of the fifth century, Jerome translated the Hebrew Tanach and the Greek New Testament into Latin, and this text (the Vulgate) became the definitive and official version used by the Roman Catholic Church.

There is evidence that the Gospel according to Matthew was originally written in Hebrew. "The church fathers Papias, Irenaeus, Origen, Eusebius, and Jerome reported that the original version of Matthew was written in Hebrew."[16] Besides being the most "Jewish" of the gospels, there are other clues as well, such as the genealogy at the beginning of the gospel that gives fourteen generations from Abraham to David (unlike the genealogy in chapter three of Luke), fourteen generations from David to the captivity in Babylon (again, unlike Luke), and fourteen generations from the captivity in Babylon to Jesus (again, unlike Luke). The reason for the forced fourteen generations was no doubt inspired by the *gematria* of the Hebrew name of David. (*Gematria* is Hebrew numerology. Each Hebrew letter is also a number. David's name in Hebrew, when added together, makes the sum of fourteen: ד = 4, ו = 6, ד = 4; 4 + 6 + 4 = 14.) A single Hebrew prototype also explains the riddle of the synoptic Gospels, which were translated from this Hebrew gospel at different times by different people.[17]

Except for a few scraps, the writings of Papias no longer exist, and what we know of his work comes from Eusebius, a fourth-century church father. Eusebius said, "Matthew composed the oracles (Logia) in the Hebrew tongue, and each man interpreted them as best he could." The Greek word, *logia*, presents some problems. It means "oracles" rather than "sayings." Perhaps,

---

[16] Alan W. Cecil, *The Noahide Code: A Guide for the Perplexed Christian*, 51.

[17] George Howard published a Hebrew Matthew in 1987, claiming that it was a fourteenth-century copy of the original Hebrew Matthew. We should note, however, that in the very first verse it had the word "Christos" spelled out phonetically in Hebrew; if this had been a first-century Jewish Matthew, it would have read "Yeshua HaMashicah," not "Yeshua HaChristos." The phonetic spelling points to Howard's manuscript as a translation from the Greek into Hebrew, rather than a Hebrew original.

like the Gospel of Thomas, the original "Matthew" was in fact a collection of Jesus's teachings. Whatever it was, we know that it was the preferred gospel among the Jewish Christians, and there were many spin-offs, such as the Gospel of the Ebionites, the Gospel of the Nazoraeans, and the Gospel of the Hebrews.

Christians like to validate the authenticity of the New Testament by the vast number of the Greek manuscripts, thumping their Christian Bibles proudly and pointing out that no other ancient document has such a well-preserved pedigree. There are indeed over five thousand Greek manuscripts of the New Testament. However, most of these date from the Middle Ages onward, a period occurring long after the texts had been edited to their proper theological contents. It is the early texts, the pre-Nicean texts instead of the later edited texts, that pose a problem for the missionary. The closer one gets to the first century and the time of the apostles, the more dissimilar the texts become. The missionary explains textual divergence as sloppiness and errors made by the scribes who copied the texts. But it stands to reason that if that were the case, the early texts would be more uniform, and as errors crept in from copyists, later texts would become more and more diverse. But it's just the opposite—the early texts are the most divergent. They only became more uniform as the scribes edited and smoothed out the language and errors of the earlier Greek texts. Still, the fact that no two texts are exactly identical in all their wording shows that the task of making the texts uniform was a task extending beyond the abilities of the Christian scribes. The problem was not that the scribes incorrectly transmitted the original writings of the apostles; the problem was *there were no "original" writings of the apostles to begin with*. It is through the writings of the church fathers that we know that the scraps of papyri found in the trash heaps were not aberrations of the "originals."

The problem with dating the ancient Greek manuscripts is that Biblical paleography is not an exact science. The papyrus and vellum manuscripts of the New Testament did not have "copyrighted by Matthew, 80 CE" written on them. Moreover, the early Christians would not think twice about writing a book and putting an apostle's name on it to give it more validity. This was a common practice back in those days. None of the gospels in the New Testament originally had the names of apostles on them; the names were added later by anonymous scribes. Dating the manuscripts takes a good deal of comparison to other papyrus fragments of that time, as well as a good deal of guesswork.

> It must [be] remembered that a manuscript could have been produced by an old scribe using a style he learned as a young man (making the manuscript appear earlier than it is), or a manuscript could have been written by a young scribe just when a certain style was nascent (making the manuscript appear later than it is). These factors could add or subtract twenty-five to fifty years to or from the date of any manuscript.[18]

Many Christian scholars have tried to push back the dating of the earliest papyri to validate apostolic authorship, sometimes even to the first century. Unfortunately, they have no hard evidence of this whatsoever, and having some nameless mid-second century scribe slap the title Matthew on a manuscript is hardly the "strong internal testimony" that Christian writers like Josh McDowell talk about.

Let us look at the two earliest scraps of Greek New Testament text we know of. Both are from the second century. One is very well known, a papyrus fragment the size of a credit card named Rylands 52. It contains a small handful of words from the Gospel of John and is touted as the earliest evidence of the gospels, tentatively dated around 125 CE. Of course, manuscript dating is far from being an exact science; most manuscripts are dated with a plus/minus twenty-five year difference, which means that the Rylands 52 papyrus could be dated anywhere from 100 CE to 150 CE. The dating of a textual fragment as small as Rylands 52 also makes the dating more problematic because the more text we have, the easier it is to date a document by comparing the text to other texts of the same era. However, there is good reason to believe that the latter date is the more accurate one.[19] This is not by the stylistic form of

---

[18] Philip W. Comfort and David P. Barrett. *The Complete Text of the Earliest New Testament Manuscripts,* Grand Rapids: Baker Books, 1999, 18.

[19] Christians claim that it would have taken a long time for John's Gospel to have been copied and

the text or "internal evidence," but by the simple fact that no one—not a single church father—ever mentions that any of the gospels existed before the mid-second century. For example, Heracleon, who was a member of the Gnostic Valentinian sect, was the first person to write about the Gospel of John in 160 CE. Irenaeus was the first "orthodox" church father to write about John, around 180 CE. When we think about the importance of the Gospel of John to Christianity, it is hard to believe that the Gospel of John was not mentioned once by any church father before 160 CE. If one takes the "eyewitness" testimony at face-value, then it is logical to believe that the Gospel of John did not exist until the mid-second century CE, especially when we consider the advanced Gnostic and theological motifs found in John's gospel.

Rylands 52 is perhaps the most famous papyrus text of the gospels and is often used by Christians to "prove" their claim that John was written in the late first century, even though Rylands 52 is dated to the mid-second century. But there is another papyrus fragment that is as old, if not older, than Rylands 52. This is a papyrus fragment called Egerton 2. Although this scrap of text is larger than the Rylands fragment and contains a good deal more text, it is hardly ever mentioned by Christians because it is from a "gospel" tradition that is unknown in any other of the five thousand Greek New Testament texts. The language of Egerton 2 is much less developed than the later traditional gospels and combines elements of Matthew, Mark, Luke, and John into its narrative. It also contains a "miracle" story that is not found in any other text of the gospels. But Christians do not like to talk about Egerton 2 because this earliest of all texts, written around the mid second century, is obviously part of an oral tradition written down before the traditions were separated into the different gospels. When Egerton 2 is added to the evidence of the disparate oral gospel quotations of the early second century church fathers, and we remember that

---

circulated from Ephesus (on the coast of modern Turkey, east of Athens) to Egypt (where Rylands 52 was found), and cite this as "proof" that the Gospel of John must have been written much earlier; say, around 90 CE or so. Of course, Paul's second missionary journey took him from Jerusalem to Antioch, across what is today Turkey, then across the Aegean Sea to Thrace, down into Greece where he visited Athens and Corinth, across the Aegean again to Ephesus, and back to Jerusalem in just three years (49–52 CE). To make the claim that it would have taken John's Gospel 35 years to make the trip from Ephesus to Egypt is an exaggeration, to put it mildly.

no church father quotes directly from any of the Gospels before the mid-second century CE, we are led to the conclusion that the gospels themselves were not written until the middle of the second century, over one hundred years after the death of Jesus.

Other early papyri that have been dated to the late second and early third centuries also show an amazing number of variances and alterations. The oral traditions of Jesus, along with "miracle stories" (many more of which never made it into the four gospels of the canonic New Testament), were woven together and edited into the four gospels we know today. The earliest gospel known is Marcion's gospel, which was based on the Gospel of Luke, minus any Old Testament references, and which was written around the middle of the second century. Although theologians claim that Marcion edited out the pro-Jewish portions, it is also highly likely that his gospel was an original creation, filled with oral teachings of Jesus and "miracle" stories. This gospel, by all accounts the first gospel written, triggered a gospel-writing frenzy among the early Christians. By the end of the second century, there were dozens of gospels floating around Christendom, including the four gospels that were later included in the New Testament.

Although Christians like to "prove" through "internal evidence" that the gospels were written in the first century, the hard evidence points to a different conclusion. Sir Frederic Kenyon's assertion that the "interval then between the dates of original composition and the earliest extant evidence becomes so small as to be in fact negligible, and the last foundation for any doubt that the [New Testament] Scriptures have come down to us substantially as they were written has now been removed" sounds forced. It is a Wizard of Oz "Pay no attention to that man behind the curtain!" plea to not look at the evidence too closely, but to trust the Christian's claims that the gospels were written in the first century based on "internal" evidence, that is, because Christians say so. But the New Testament itself speaks of epistles that were forged in Paul's name. In 2 Thessalonians 2:1–2, we read, "Now we beseech you, brethren, by the coming of our Lord Jesus Christ, and by our gathering together unto him, that ye be not soon shaken in mind, or be troubled, neither by spirit, nor by word, **nor by letter as from us**, as that the day of Christ is at hand" (emphasis added).

For most of the history of Christianity, one of the bulwarks of its theology was the uniformity and inerrancy of the text of the New Testament. From the start of the Middle Ages, the Roman Catholic Church—and its later offshoots, the Protestant and Eastern Orthodox churches—used the Byzantine text, which is familiar to us as the King James Version of the Christian Bible. Christianity built an elaborate defense of its faith based on this text. Christians memorized their favorite verses, such as 1 John 5:7–8, "the Father, the Word, and the Holy Ghost: and these three are one. And there are three that bear witness in earth" and Acts 8:37, "And Philip said, If you believe with all your heart, you may. And he answered and said, I believe that Jesus Christ is the Son of God." Whenever a Christian debated a non-Christian, either a Noahide or a Jew, he could, like a guard dog protecting his theology, trot out these faithful verses to "prove" Christian claims of the trinity and Jesus's divinity. After all, it had to be true. It said so, right there in the New Testament.

The knowledge most Christians have about how the New Testament was written is negligible at best. The soothing mantra that the theologians and biblical scholars chant with their near-Masonic fervor—*there is nothing wrong with the early Greek texts, they are completely trustworthy*—has forced scholars to work from the assumption that the gospels were written by the apostles themselves and copied from first-century originals. Instead of going to the primary sources of the New Testament, Christians rely on the words of their scholars and theologians. There is, however, no level at which the New Testament—the Greek texts, the translation, or the interpretation—does not have major problems.

The Primary Sources

A few words need to be said about the primary sources. There is a difference between primary and secondary sources. A primary source is a document from an eyewitness to the events being recorded, or at least from the time of the events. Theologians often speak of the witnesses, or the original writings of the apostles such as Matthew, John, and Peter. The problem is that we do not have these originals. We do not even have the copies of the originals.[20] What we have, as far as the New Testament is concerned, are a handful of papyrus documents, vellum codices, and writings of the early Church Fathers. These documents, which are the true primary sources, are the bottom line, the authentic texts of the New Testament book of Matthew. We cannot argue about the "inerrant original" book supposedly written by Matthew. It does not exist and, by all evidence, never did exist. There are no other early texts besides these, no other eyewitnesses, no other "experts" we can summon up to refute what these early texts say (or in many cases what they do *not* say). Also, we must keep in mind that although there are over five thousand Greek manuscripts of the New Testament, the vast majority of those manuscripts were written *after* the fourth century, and even the two most important early manuscripts—Sinaiticus and Vaticanus—were written after the Council of Nicea in 325 CE. To put this in perspective, remember that the length of time between the first of Paul's Epistles (around 49 CE) and the Council of Nicea (325) was 276 years. This is the same span of time between the year George Washington was born (1732) to Barack Obama's election (2008). If we consider all the history and changes that have happened in America since 1732, we can better appreciate the historical importance of these early manuscripts. The following list gives the primary sources of the Gospel of Matthew.

---

[20] "How does it help us to say that the [New Testament] is the inerrant word of God if in fact we don't have the words that God inerrantly inspired, but only the words copied by the scribes — sometimes correctly but sometimes (many times!) incorrectly? What good is it to say that the autographs (i.e., the originals) were inspired? We don't have the originals! We have only error-ridden copies, and the vast majority of these are centuries removed from the originals and different from them, evidently, in thousands of ways." Bart D Ehrman, *Misquoting Jesus,* San Francisco: HarperSanFransisco, 2005, 7.

Papyrus

This is the list of the earliest and most important manuscripts we have for Matthew. The first manuscripts we have are the papyrus manuscripts, designated with a 𝔭. Papyrus comes from tall sedge plant with a triangular stem whose pith was used in ancient Egypt to make a type of paper. This paper was a popular writing material in the early centuries of the Common Era. Fewer than sixty papyri manuscripts of the New Testament, most containing only a few verses, can be dated before the fourth century. The papyri manuscripts were found in Egypt, where the dry desert climate was conducive to their preservation. The following are the papyri that contain the Gospel of Matthew:

𝔭^1—Written around the middle of the third century, about the year 250. Discovered in a trash heap in Oxyrhynchus, Egypt. This manuscript consists of only one sheet, about six by ten inches. It contains Matthew 1:1–9, 12, 14–20.

𝔭^{35}—From Oxyrhynchus, Egypt. Written around the beginning of the fourth century. Matthew 25:12–15, 20–23. The text of this papyrus is what theologians call a "mixed text," which is another way of saying that it still bore the marks of an oral tradition.

𝔭^{37}—Obtained in Cairo, Egypt, in 1924. Written around the end of the third century. Matthew 26:19–52. It is called a "free" text (another term for a "mixed text").

𝔭^{45}—Unknown origin; somewhere in Egypt. Early third century. Matthew 20:24–32; 21:13–19; 25:41–46; 26:1–39. "Partly Alexandrian, partly Western (pre-Caesarean) text."[21] The scribe responsible for this text paraphrased extensively, with different text-types in each book (Matthew, Mark, Luke, John, and Acts).

𝔭^{53}—Middle of the third century. Unknown, but most likely from Fayum, Egypt. Matthew 26:29–40. Egyptian "mixed text."

𝔭^{64}—Beginning of the third century, about 200, found in Coptos

---

[21] Bruce M. Metzger, *The Text of the New Testament: Its Transmission, Corruption, and Restoration.* New York: Oxford University Press, 1980, 37.

(Qift), Egypt. This manuscript consists of three small scraps of text containing a few words from Matthew 26:7, 10, 14–15, 22–23, 31–33. 𝔓⁶⁴ has an Alexandrian slant to the text.

𝔓⁶⁷—Same as 𝔓⁶⁴. The two texts were originally part of the same manuscript. Matthew 3:9–15, 20–22, 25–28.

𝔓⁷⁰—Third century, from Oxyrhynchus, Egypt. Matthew 2:13–16; 2:22–3:1; 11:26–27; 12:4–5; 24:3–6, 12–15. 𝔓⁷⁰ is a "sloppy" text.

𝔓⁷⁷—Late second century, from Oxyrhynchus, Egypt. From the same manuscript as Matthew 23:30–39. A mixed text.

𝔓⁸⁶—About 300. Matthew 5:13–16, 22–25. Text agrees with B.

𝔓¹⁰¹—Third century, from Oxyrhynchus, Egypt. Matthew 3:10–12; 3:16–4:3. Another "proto-Alexandrian," meaning it is a mixed text.

𝔓¹⁰²—Late third or early fourth century, from Oxyrhynchus, Egypt. Matthew 4:11–12, 22–23.

𝔓¹⁰³—From the same manuscript as 𝔓⁷⁷. Matthew 13:55–57.

𝔓¹⁰⁴—Mid-second century, from Oxyrhynchus, Egypt. Matthew 21:34–37, 43, 45(?). This very small scrap of text does not include one verse, Matthew 21:44.

𝔓^Antinoopolis **2.54**—Third century. Matthew 6:10-12, earliest extant copy of the Lord's Prayer. May have been used as an amulet.

Early Uncials

An uncial is an early Greek text written in capital letters. These manuscripts were written on vellum, which is a skin of an animal (such as a sheep or antelope) and prepared for writing.

0171—Late third century. Matthew 10:17–23, 25–32. Western text.

א—Codex Sinaiticus. The earliest complete New Testament text (also contains the noncanonical Shepherd of Hermes and Epistle of Barnabas). Written about 350 CE. Mixed Alexandrian/Western text. This is the oldest complete manuscript of the New Testament we have. There are over 14,000 "corrections" in the text.

A—Codex Alexandrinus. Early fifth century. Originally contained Old and New Testaments, plus First and Second Clement and Psalms of Solomon. Matthew 1:1–25:6 is missing, as well as John 6:50–8:52 and 2 Corinthians 4:13–12:6. The text is Byzantine in the gospels and Alexandrian in the Pauline epistles.

B—Codex Vaticanus. Fourth century. Originally had all of the New Testament, but it is now missing Hebrews 9:14–13:25, the pastoral Epistles, Philemon, and the Apocalypse. The text is Alexandrian; in fact, this is the text that is the foundation for the Alexandrian text supporters. This text has also been corrupted by a corrector, "who traced over every letter afresh, omitting only those letters and words which he believed to be incorrect."[22] One interesting note about Codex Vaticanus: the epistle of 2 Peter is absent, hinting that even in the fourth century, the authorship and authenticity of 2 Peter were disputed.

C—Codex Ephraemi. Early fifth century. Very important text, but quite mixed, which means that in the beginning of the fifth century, there was still not a uniform text, such as the Byzantine. Two later correctors also worked on this manuscript and made changes in the text.

D—Codex Bezae. Fifth-century western text with many original readings, written in both Greek and Latin. In Acts 15:20 and 29 it omits "and from things strangled," having instead Hillel's negative form of the "Golden Rule" (*Shabbat* 31a).

E—Codex Basiliensis. Eighth-century Byzantine text.

---
[22] Metzger, *The Text of the New Testament*, 47.

Eᵃ—Codex E². An early seventh century text. Mixed text with both Western and Byzantine readings. This manuscript contains the earliest text of Acts 8:37.

W—Codex Washington. Late fourth century. Mixed text.

Θ—Codex Koridethi. Eighth century. The text is Caesarean in Mark, Byzantine in the other gospels.

Minuscules

These are later Greek texts written in a "cursive" Greek.

λ—The Lake group. A group of similar texts first identified by Kirsopp Lake in the early twentieth century.

Φ—The Ferrar Group. A group of texts with similar wording; for instance, this family of texts has the pericope from John 7:53–8:11 (the woman taken in adultery) in the gospel of Luke.

𝕂—Koine. These are the Byzantine texts, the standardized texts of the church from the late fourth century onwards.

Other Early Versions of the New Testament

These are other versions of the gospels that were translated into different languages.

sy—The Syriac text. Five different versions are known. They are from the Western text group.

it—Old Latin. Scholars believe that the Old Latin manuscripts date from the late second century. They are usually written in the Western text.

cop—Coptic text. Coptic is a late form of the ancient Egyptian language. Two dialects of the Coptic text are:
sa—Sahidic
bo—Bohairic.

vg — The Vulgate. Latin translation by Jerome in the late fourth century.

Note that other ancient versions of the New Testament exist such as the Armenian, Georgian, Ethiopic, and Slavonic versions.

Early Church Fathers

Clement of Rome—Earliest church father whose writings have survived. Lived from the late first to early second century. In his epistle 1 Clement, he quotes often from the Tanach, and the quotes are "frequently introduced by such well-known formulas as 'the Scripture says'…'it is written'…'that which is written'"[23] His few quotes from the gospels are from oral tradition, not the written text. His quotes of Paul's epistles are more definite, which presupposes that the written epistles of Paul were known then, but not the written gospels.

Ignatius—Early second century. He wrote seven letters, which are in three different forms: long, longer, and longest. The argument as to whether the seven letters of Ignatius are genuine has raged for many years. His writing has echoes of Pauline and Johannine elements.

Marcion—Mid-second century. Excommunicated in 144 CE as a heretic, Marcion is responsible for putting together the first New Testament (consisting of the Gospel of Luke, and many of Paul's epistles). These were edited by the anti-Semitic Marcion, who removed all *Tanach* references.

---

[23] Metzger, *The Canon of the New Testament.* Oxford: Clarendon Press, 1992, 41.

Justin—Mid-second century.

Tatian—Mid-second century. responsible for writing the Diatessaron, a "harmony" of the gospels. "Marcion and Tatian undoubtedly had a certain corrupting influence upon the transmission of the New Testament text."[24] The Church has never desired to investigate this "corrupting influence."

Irenaeus—Late second century.

Theodotus—Late second century. Another "heretic" according to the mainstream heretics.

Tertullian—Early third century.

Clement of Alexandria—Early third century.

Origen—Early third century. Castrated himself when he was a young man so he would not be tempted to sin, which demonstrates how well he understood the Torah. A prolific writer, he had a habit of always paraphrasing verses from the New Testament, but seldom repeated the same verse exactly. Suspected of writing (or, at the very least) editing the Septuagint.

Hippolytus—Early third century.

Cyprian—Mid-third century.

Eusebius—Early fourth century.

Epiphanius—Fourth century.

Didymus—Late fourth century. Follower of the teachings of Origen.

Chrysostom—Late fourth century. The viciousness of his

---

[24] Metzger, *The Text of the New Testament*, 142.

anti-Semitic attacks on Jews stands out even among the other anti-Semitic church fathers.[25] His teachings greatly influenced Christian theology.

Jerome—Late fourth, early fifth century. Translated the Hebrew and Greek texts into Latin. Jerome's Latin version is now known as the Vulgate.

---

[25] "What is this disease? The festivals of the pitiful and miserable Jews are soon to march upon us one after the other and in quick succession: the feast of Trumpets, the feast of Tabernacles, the fasts. There are many in our ranks who say they think as we do. Yet some of these are going to watch the festivals and others will join the Jews in keeping their feasts and observing their fasts. I wish to drive this perverse custom from the Church right now. My homilies against the Anomians can be put off to another time, and the postponement would cause no harm. But now that the Jewish festivals are close by and at the very door, if I should fail to cure those who are sick with the Judaizing disease." (John Chrysostom, Homily 1.)

Matthew

Chapter I

1. The book of the generation[1] of Jesus[2] Christ, the son of David, the son of Abraham. 2. Abraham begat Isaac; and Isaac begat Jacob; and Jacob begat Judas and his brethren; 3. And Judas begat Phares and Zara of Thamar; and Phares begat Esrom; and Esrom begat Aram; 4. And Aram begat Aminadab; and Aminadab begat Naasson; and Naasson begat Salmon; 5. And Salmon begat Booz of Rachab; and Booz begat Obed of Ruth; and Obed begat Jesse; 6. And Jesse begat David the king; and David the king begat Solomon of her that had been the wife of Urias; 7. And Solomon begat Roboam; and Roboam begat Abia; and Abia begat Asa; 8. And Asa[3] begat Josaphat; and Josaphat begat Joram; and Joram begat Ozias; 9. And Ozias begat Joatham; and

---

[1] 1:1. *The book of the generation of Jesus Christ.* The gospel of Matthew begins with the genealogy of Jesus in an attempt to legitimize Jesus's claim to the kingship of Israel. This genealogy of Joseph's line is different from the genealogy of Joseph in Luke (cf. Luke 3:23), not only in the names of the descendants, but also in the number of generations (Luke has forty–three generations between David and Jesus, Matthew has only twenty–eight). The problem that Christianity faced was that if Joseph was not Jesus's father, and a descendant of the line of David, then Jesus could not possibly have been the Messiah. Christianity often presented the argument that since God was the father of Abraham, Isaac, and Jacob, then God was the "father" of Judah, too, and therefore of the line of David. Of course, the problem with this argument is that this would make God the father of other tribes of Israel as well, tribes such as Dan, or Benjamin, and Naphtali. The early Greek texts of Matthew (cf. comm. v. 16) say that Joseph was the father of Jesus, and that Joseph and Mary were married. These texts were later altered to support the "virgin birth" concept of the church, a concept that was not supported by Paul or the earliest church fathers, and is certainly not supported by Judaism.

[2] 1. Iησοῦ — "Jesus." This is the Greek translation for the popular Jewish name *Yeshua*, which is the shortened form of *Yehoshua* (Joshua), the Hebrew who took over from Moses and led the Jews into the promised land (cf. Hebrews 4:8). Since the English language, as we know it today, would not come into existence for well over a thousand years after Jesus's death, it is certain that "Jesus" never heard the word "Jesus" during his lifetime. By the same token, we do not speak of "Isaac" Rabin or "Moses" Dayan, even though "Isaac" is the English form of Yitshak and "Moses" is the English form of Moshe. It is ironic that so many Christians pray in the "name" of Jesus, yet do not know his real name.

[3] 8. *Asa.* The earliest manuscripts we have of Matthew, most notably Sinaiticus, Vaticanus, and 𝔭[1] have the name *Asaph* instead of *Asa*.

Joatham begat Achaz; and Achaz begat Ezekias; 10. And Ezekias begat Manasses; and Manasses begat Amon; and Amon[4] *begat Josias; 11. And Josias begat Jechonias and his brethren, about the time they were carried away to Babylon: 12. And after they were brought to Babylon, Jechonias begat Salathiel; and Salathiel begat Zorobabel; 13. And Zorobabel begat Abiud; and Abiud begat Eliakim; and Eliakim begat Azor; 14. And Azor begat Sadoc; and Sadoc begat Achim; and Achim begat Eliud; 15. And Eliud begat Eleazar; and Eleazar begat Matthan; and Matthan begat Jacob; 16. And Jacob begat Joseph the husband of Mary, of whom was born* Jesus, *who is called Christ.*[5] *17. So all the generations*

---

[4] 10. *Amon.* Early manuscripts have the name *Amos* instead of *Amon.*

[5] 16. *And Jacob begat Joseph the husband of Mary, of whom was born Jesus, who is called Christ.* In the nearly five thousand Greek manuscripts containing Matthew, there are many thousands of variations in the Greek texts, so many that no two manuscripts are exactly alike. Every verse in the Gospel of Matthew has some sort of textual variance, and space requires that we cite only a small percentage of the many thousands of alterations (many verses of Matthew have dozens of different versions). Christians claim that no theological concepts are affected by the textual corruption of the Greek texts of the New Testament, and that the "vast majority" of the alterations consist of innocent and insignificant changes in words such as "the" or "and." This argument is refuted by the textual alterations in the very first chapter of the very first book of the New Testament, where the Greek text and the English translation have been changed to obfuscate the theological problem that Joseph was Jesus's biological father, which would negate the theological teaching of the "virgin birth." It should also be noted that whenever there are more than two variations in a certain text, it was not a simple "scribal error," but that the text was heavily edited. It could also be a piece of oral tradition that was inserted later.

The earliest and most reliable Greek texts of Matthew imply that Jesus was the son of Joseph and that Joseph and Mary were husband and wife, not merely engaged. The later texts were altered to support the theological teaching that Joseph was not Jesus's father and that Joseph and Mary were not yet married before Jesus's birth. Here are some of the variations found in the Greek manuscripts for Matthew 1:16:

> *Jacob the father of Joseph the husband of Mary, of whom Jesus was born, who is called the Messiah*: 𝔓¹, ℵ, B, C, W, λ, 𝔎, it (some MSS.), vg, sy^p, sa, Tertullian
>
> *Jacob the father of Joseph, to whom the virgin Mary having betrothed bore Jesus who is called Christ*: Θ, Φ, it (some MSS.)

from Abraham to David are fourteen[6] *generations and from David until the carrying away into Babylon are fourteen generations; and from the carrying away into Babylon unto Christ are fourteen generations. 18. Now the birth of Jesus Christ*[7] *was on this wise: When as his mother Mary was espoused to Joseph,*[8] *before they*

> Jacob the father of Joseph. Joseph, to whom was betrothed the virgin Mary, was the father of Jesus who is called the Christ: sy[s]
>
> Jacob the father of Joseph, to whom was betrothed the virgin Mary who (fem.) bore Jesus the Christ: sy[c]
>
> Jacob the father of Joseph the husband of Mary who bore Jesus who is called Christ: bo

[6] 17. *fourteen generations.* In order to have "fourteen" generations from David to the deportation to Babylon, four kings were left out of the list: Ahaziah the son of Jehoram, Joash the son of Ahaziah, Amaziah the son of Joash, and Jehoiakim the son of Josiah (cf. 1 Chronicles 3:10–16). Also note that Uzziah and Azariah were the same person (cf. 2 Kings 14:21 and 2 Chronicles 26:1).

[7] 18. *Now the birth of Jesus Christ was on this wise.* Sinaiticus, ף[1], and other early Greek texts have *Jesus the Messiah*; Vaticanus has *Christ Jesus*, the old Italic and other texts have *Christ*, and Codex W has *Jesus*. The theological interpretation of Matthew 1:18–20 is that before Joseph and Mary were married, he found her expecting a child and decided to divorce her, only privately so as not to humiliate her. But an angel told him in a dream not to worry; the child was conceived of the Holy Spirit, and Joseph should go ahead and marry her. This interpretation is better suited to the story in Luke, which gives a different series of events. The problem of the forced interpretation is compounded by the insertion of words into the text that are not in the ancient Greek manuscripts (cf. commentary to verse 20).

[8] 18. *was espoused to Joseph.* The Greek word for "espoused" is μνηστευθείσης, which means literally "to give a souvenir or engagement present." This is different from the word used for "espouse" in 2 Corinthians 11:2, which is ἡρμοσάμην, or to "betroth." According to the Talmud (*Sanhedrin* 21a), a woman must be married with a *kesubah*, which is a document that provides for a marriage settlement (the three ways for a Jewish man to be legally married are with a formal document, a transfer of money, or sexual relations). The text states that Mary was Joseph's legal wife, not his espoused wife-to-be, for in verses 16 and 19, it clearly says that Joseph was Mary's husband, and they are referred to as husband and wife throughout the rest of the gospel. If they were truly God-fearing, observant Jews, they would not be allowed to be alone together and certainly not allowed to live together if they had merely been engaged, and since there is no mention of their being married between verses 18 and 19, it is clear that they were already married at the beginning of the gospel.

came together, she was found with child of the Holy Ghost. 19. Then Joseph her husband, being a just man, and not willing to make her a publick example, was minded to put her away privily. 20. But while he thought on these things, behold, the angel of the Lord appeared unto him in a dream,[9] *saying, Joseph, thou son of David, fear not to take unto thee Mary thy wife:*[10] *for that which is conceived in her is of the Holy Ghost 21. And she shall bring forth a son, and thou shalt call his name JESUS: for he shall save his people from their sins. 22. Now all this was done, that it might be*

---

[9] 20. *the angel of the Lord appeared unto him in a dream.* This also occurs in Matthew 2:13, 19, and 22. God speaking to people in dreams and foretelling future events signifies that the person is a prophet. It is odd that very little is made of this, as Jesus's being the son of a known prophet would certainly be of greater public relations value than Jesus the adopted son of an incompetent carpenter (cf. commentary to Matthew 8:2). We have to ask: Who made Joseph a prophet? Did he appear before the Sanhedrin as required? Why was Joseph never mentioned as a prophet? In the few places in the gospels where Joseph is mentioned, he is never called a prophet, and it is with disbelief that Jesus could be the Messiah when he was simply the son of an ordinary man (cf. Luke 4:22). It should also be pointed out that nowhere in Luke is Joseph mentioned as having any sort of prophetic visions. Mary (Jesus's mother, who is not mentioned in Matthew as having any prophetic visions) and Zacharias, the father of John the Baptist, were, however, given the status of prophets.

[10] 20. *Joseph ... fear not to take unto thee Mary thy wife.* "Thy wife," not "thy betrothed." The word used for "take" in verse 20, "do not be afraid to take Miriam home as your wife," is the Greek word παραλαβεῖν, from the two Greek words παρά (para, "beside," as in the word "parallel") and λαμβάνω (lambano, "to take"). In other New Testament uses of the word παραλαβεῖν, such as Luke 9:28, "Jesus ... took Peter, John, and James with him" (NIV) or in Matthew 18:16, *"take one or two others along"* (NIV) it has this meaning to "take someone alongside." Nowhere else in the New Testament does it take on the connotation of "to marry" that it has in Matthew 1:20. In order to make sure the theological interpretation of the word παραλαβεῖν as "to marry" is clear, words have been deliberately added to the English text, words that are not in the original Greek. The following examples show how this was done. The underlined words in the English translations are not found in the Greek text:
  fear not to take <u>unto thee</u> Mary thy wife (KJV)
  do not be afraid to take Miriam <u>as</u> your wife (NASV)
  do not be afraid to take Miriam <u>home as</u> your wife (NIV)

This addition of excess words not found in the Greek text occurs again in verse 24, again with the word παραλαβεῖν, where the text reads as *take with you Miriam your wife.*

fulfilled which was spoken of the Lord by the prophet, saying, 23. Behold, a virgin shall be with child,[11] and shall bring forth a son, and they shall call his name Emmanuel, which being interpreted is, God with us. 24. Then Joseph being raised from sleep did as the angel of the Lord had bidden him,[12] and took unto him his wife:

---

[11] *23. Behold, a virgin shall be with child.* As with the other quotes in the New Testament, the first quotation from the *Tanach* (which Christians call the Old Testament) has been taken from the Septuagint version of Isaiah 7:14 and is taken out of context. The New Testament has the word παρθένος, or "virgin." The Hebrew word, from Isaiah 7:14, is עלמה (*almah*) which means "young woman," not "virgin." The Hebrew word for "virgin" is בתולה (*bethulah*). The "sign" mentioned in Isaiah 7:14 was given to Ahaz, seven hundred years before the events in the New Testament transpired. Since the verb הרה (*harah*) used with עלמה is in the present tense, along with the use of the definite article (*the* young woman), this indicates that this person was someone Isaiah and Ahaz both knew. As for the name Emmanuel, this is the only place in the entire New Testament where this name is mentioned. Jesus was never called Emmanuel. Since the Christian claim of Jesus's authority is based upon his supposed "divine" nature, and this "divine" nature is based upon the virgin birth, this is a crucial distinction.

[12] *24. Then Joseph being raised from sleep did as the angel of the Lord had bidden him.* The Talmud (*Ketubbot* 9b) tells of the tradition (begun in the time of David) of how married men going off to war or on a dangerous journey secretly gave their wives papers for divorce. Since the Law clearly says that a woman whose husband had no witnesses to his death cannot remarry, she could hold onto these papers until she was sure that her husband was dead, then produce them and obtain a divorce. This is, more than likely, what Joseph wanted to do, and why the account in Matthew calls him "just." He wanted to make sure that, in the event of his death, Mary could remarry and be provided for. Where and why was Joseph traveling? Both the text and tradition are obscure. Luke 2:1–3 tells of a census, but there is no other historical record of this ever taking place. Why would Joseph leave a very pregnant wife to fend for herself to go on a dangerous journey? Next to the census story (of which there is no other proof of its ever happening), the most probable explanation concerns the three festivals every year for which all Jewish males were required to travel to Jerusalem. Joseph, being "a just man," would have kept this law. At the time, hundreds of Jewish men were crucified along the roads of Galilee by the vengeful Romans, for it was during this time that a rebellion led by Judas of Galilee was going on (cf. Josephus, *Wars of the Jews*, 2:8:1 and 17:8.) Joseph probably feared that the Romans would find him at the wrong place at the wrong time and nail him to a tree.

The narrative of Matthew 1:18–20 can thus be explained like this: Before Joseph and his wife Miriam went on a journey together, she became pregnant.

25. And knew her not till she had brought forth her firstborn[13] *son: and he called his name JESUS.*

Because of her pregnancy, and due to the volatile situation in Galilee, Joseph decided to go alone, and in case he did not return, he privately gave her papers for divorce, as was the custom when a husband was forced to make a dangerous journey or go off to war. This was to assure that, in case of the lack of any witnesses to his death, Miriam could remarry. Before Joseph left, however, an angel spoke to him in a dream and told him that it was safe to take his wife with him on the journey. This account from the Noahide perspective certainly makes more sense than the Christian theological explanation. It should also be noted that Matthew does not say that Joseph traveled from Nazareth to Bethlehem; that tradition is from Luke 2:4.

[13] 25. *her firstborn son.* The word "firstborn" was added to the Greek text centuries later because of the theological teaching of the "virgin birth." The earliest and most important texts, such as Sinaiticus and Vaticanus, omit "firstborn."

until she had borne a son. ℵ, B, λ, φ, it, sy^c, sa, bo
her firstborn son: 𝕂, C, D, W, vg, sy^p. The Sinaitic Syraic (sy^s) has *she bore to him (Joseph) a son* (cf. commentary to 1:16).

II

1. Now when Jesus was born in Bethlehem of Judaea in the days of Herod the king, behold, there came wise men from the east to Jerusalem,[1] *2. Saying, Where is he that Is born King of the Jews? for we have seen his star in the east, and are come to worship him.*[2] *3. When Herod the king had heard these things, he was troubled, and all Jerusalem with him. 4. And when he had gathered all the chief priests and scribes of the people together, he demanded of them where Christ should be born. 5. And they said unto him, In Bethlehem of Judaea: for thus it is written by the prophet, 6. And*

---

[1] *2:1. there came wise men from the east to Jerusalem.* The Greek word μάγοι ("magi") is the root of the word "magician." The magi were pagan astrologers, cf. Deuteronomy 18:14. Also see Acts 13:6, where the same word is used for "sorcerer." Clement of Rome, the earliest Ante-Nicene church father whose writings are still extant, said in his epistle to Corinthians (chapter 25), "Let us consider that wonderful sign [of the resurrection] which takes place in eastern lands, that is, in Arabia and the countries round about. There is a certain bird which is called a phœnix. This is the only one of its kind, and lives five hundred years. And when the time of its dissolution draws near that it must die, it builds itself a nest of frankincense, and myrrh, and other spices, into which, when the time is fulfilled, it enters and dies. But as the flesh decays a certain kind of worm is produced, which, being nourished by the juices of the dead bird, brings forth feathers. Then, when it has acquired strength, it takes up that nest in which are the bones of its parent, and bearing these it passes from the land of Arabia into Egypt, to the city called Heliopolis. And, in open day, flying in the sight of all men, it places them on the altar of the sun, and having done this, hastens back to its former abode. The priests then inspect the registers of the dates, and find that it has returned exactly as the five hundredth year was completed." Here is the pagan fable about the phœnix, its death and rebirth, and its "nest" of frankincense and myrrh, all used allegorically regarding Jesus. Because this letter by Clement (around 100 CE) was written before the appearance of the "virgin birth" story in Matthew, it seems likely that this myth had an influence on the "virgin birth" narrative.

[2] *2. and are come to worship him.* The word "worship" in Greek is προσκυνῆσαι, from πρός ("towards"), and κύων ("dog"): "to crouch as a dog." This word implies simply to bow down as a form of greeting and respect, as is the norm in many cultures. It is telling that the first visitors to fawn upon the baby Jesus were pagan idolaters.

thou Bethlehem, in the land of Judah,[3] *art not the least among the princes of Judah: for out of thee shall come a Governor, that shall rule my people Israel. 7. Then Herod, when he had privily called the wise men, enquired of them diligently what time the star appeared. 8. And he sent them to Bethlehem, and said, Go and search diligently for the young child; and when ye have found him, bring me word again, that I may come and worship him also. 9. When they had heard the king, they departed; and, lo, the star, which they saw in the east, went before them, till it came and stood over where the young child was. 10. When they saw the star, they rejoiced with exceeding great joy. 11. And when they were come into the house,*[4] *they saw the young child with Mary his mother, and fell down, and worshipped him: and when they had opened their treasures, they presented unto him gifts; gold, and frankincense, and myrrh. 12. And being warned of God in a dream that they should not return to Herod, they departed into their own country another way. 13. And when they were departed, behold, the angel of the Lord appeareth to Joseph in a dream, saying, Arise, and take the young child and his mother, and flee into Egypt,*[5] *and be thou there until I bring thee word: for Herod will seek the young child to destroy him. 14. When he arose, he took the young child and his mother by night, and departed into Egypt: 15. And was there until the death of Herod: that it might be fulfilled which was spoken of*

---

[3] 6. *And thou Bethlehem, in the land of Judah.* This verse from Micah 5:1 in the Tanach needs to be read in its correct context. The next verse (Micah 5:2) says, "Therefore, He (God) will deliver them (to their enemies) until the time that a woman in childbirth gives birth; then the rest of his brothers will return with the Children of Israel." This teaches that the exile will be as hard as the labor pains of a woman in childbirth, but that it will result in the rebirth of the Jewish nation.

[4] 11. *And when they were come into the house.* Unlike many of the paintings and scenes depicting the magi visiting Jesus in a manger, the writer of Matthew has Jesus in a house, not a stable.

[5] 13. *flee into Egypt. Rashi*, in his commentary on Genesis 26:2, explains that God forbade Isaac from going down into Egypt because he had been consecrated as an offering. This raises a problem with the theological viewpoint that Jesus was consecrated as an offering before he was born, since his trip to Egypt would invalidate his status as an offering for the "sins of the world."

the Lord by the prophet, saying, Out of Egypt have I called my son.[6] 16. Then Herod, when he saw that he was mocked of the wise men, was exceeding wroth, and sent forth, and slew all the children that were in Bethlehem, and in all the coasts thereof, from two years old and under, according to the time which he had diligently enquired of the wise men. 17. Then was fulfilled that which was spoken[7] by Jeremy the prophet, saying, 18. In Rama was there a voice heard,[8] lamentation, and weeping, and great mourning, Rachel[9] weeping for her children, and would not be comforted, because they are not. 19. But when Herod was dead, behold, an angel of the Lord appeareth in a dream to Joseph in Egypt, 20. Saying, Arise, and take the young child and his mother, and go into the land of Israel: for they are dead which sought the young child's life. 21. And he arose, and took the young child and his mother, and came into the land of Israel. 22. But when he heard that Archelaus did reign in Judaea in the room of his father Herod, he was afraid to go thither: notwithstanding, being warned of God in a dream, he turned aside into the parts of Galilee: 23. And he came and dwelt in a city called Nazareth: that it might be fulfilled which was spoken by the prophets, He shall be called a Nazarene.[10]

---

[6] 15. *Out of Egypt have I called my son.* This quote from Hosea 11:1 is also taken out of context. The entire verse in the *Tanach* reads: "When Israel was a lad, I loved him, and since Egypt I have been calling out to My son." This is a reference to Israel and the Exodus, not Jesus. This is one of the verses that Christians teach can only be understood via a "spiritual" (i.e., Gnostic) interpretation.

[7] 17. *Then was fulfilled that which was spoken.* There is no record of the murder of children by Herod in any other verifiable source. This is an attempt to draw a parallel between Jesus and Moses.

[8] 18. *In Rama was there a voice heard. Rashi* comments that Jeremiah 31:14 is about Rachel pleading with God about bringing idols into the temple (2 Kings 21:4–5), reminding Him about her generosity of spirit when she did not protest when Leah was fraudulently married to Jacob. God acquiesced to her plea and promised that Israel would eventually be redeemed by her merit.

[9] 18. *Rachel.* The lines of Judah (i.e., Jesus) and Levi (i.e., John the Baptist) did not come from Rachel. Judah and Levi were the children of Leah (Genesis 29:34–35) which makes this "prophecy" irrelevant.

[10] 23. *He shall be called a Nazarene.* This "prophecy," as given here, does not exist anywhere in the Hebrew Scriptures. One of the claims of Christianity is

that Jesus "fulfilled" prophetic scriptures of the Old Testament, but all of these "prophecies" are inventions of the early church and are either taken out of context or, like this one, simply made up later by anonymous Christian scribes (cf. Matthew 27:9–10, John 7:37–38, James 4:5).

III

1. In those days¹ came John the Baptist, preaching in the wilderness of Judaea, 2. And saying, Repent ye: for the kingdom of heaven is at hand. 3. For this is he that was spoken of by the prophet Esaias,² saying, The voice of one crying in the wilderness, Prepare ye the way of the Lord, make his paths straight. 4. And the same John had his raiment of camel's hair, and a leathern girdle about his loins;³ and his meat was locusts⁴ and wild honey. 5. Then went out to him Jerusalem,⁵ and all Judaea, and all the region round about Jordan, 6. And were baptized of him in Jordan, confessing their sins. 7.

---

[1] 3:1. *In those days.* The narrative in Matthew suddenly jumps thirty years from Jesus's infancy to his baptism by John. The reason for this "silent period" is that Matthew originally began at chapter 3 with his baptism, as do the gospels of Mark and John and the earliest version of Luke in Marcion's New Testament. The earliest versions of Matthew, such as the Gospel of the Nazareans and the Gospel of the Ebionites used by the early Jewish Christian churches, do not have the virgin birth story. "Epiphanius (late fourth century Church father) incorrectly entitles this [Gospel of the Ebionites] the "Hebrew" gospel, and alleges that it is an abridged, truncated version of the Gospel of Matthew." [*The Other Gospels: Non-Canonical Gospel Texts*. Ron Cameron, ed. (Philadelphia: The Westminster Press, 1982), 103.] The entire "virgin birth" narrative of the first two chapters, beginning with the angel of God telling Joseph (or, in Luke, Mary) that they would have a son and ending with the proclamation of Jesus being a "Nazarene," sounds suspiciously like the story of Samson in Judges 13. Unlike a true Nazir, however, Jesus drank wine, which would disqualify him from being a Nazir as was Samson.

[2] 3. *spoken of by the prophet Esaias.* A passage from Isaiah 40:3. Here we have the first use in the Greek translation of the Hebrew of the name *HaShem*, or the Holy Name of God (also known as the tetragrammaton). The context in Isaiah is that a heavenly voice is heard announcing to prepare a highway in the desert to make the return of the exiles from Babylon easier. The Gnostic interpretation links this verse with John the Baptizer.

[3] 4. *and a leathern girdle about his loins.* Cf. 2 Kings 1:8. This is an attempt to portray John the Baptist as Elijah. This contradicts John 1:21, where John says he is *not* Elijah.

[4] 4. *and his meat was locusts.* According to *Rashi*, the edible insects mentioned in Leviticus 11:22 were a type of locust, but by *Rashi's* time scholars were unable to identify them.

[5] 5. *Then went out to him Jerusalem.* Epiphanius's *Against Heresies* (xxx.13:4) says that the Gospel of the Ebionites has *John was baptizing, and Pharisees went out to him.*

But when he saw many of the Pharisees and Sadducees come to his baptism, he said unto them, O generation of vipers, who hath warned you to flee from the wrath to come? 8. Bring forth therefore fruits meet for repentance: 9. And think not to say within yourselves, We have Abraham to our father: for I say unto you, that God is able of these stones to raise up children unto Abraham. 10. And now also the axe is laid unto the root of the trees: therefore every tree which bringeth not forth good fruit is hewn down, and cast into the fire. 11. I indeed baptize you with water unto repentance: but he that cometh after me is mightier than I, whose shoes I am not worthy to bear: he shall baptize you with the Holy Ghost, and with fire: 12. Whose fan is in his hand, and he will thoroughly purge his floor, and gather his wheat into the garner; but he will burn up the chaff with unquenchable fire. 13. Then cometh Jesus from Galilee to Jordan unto John, to be baptized of him.[6] 14. But John forbad him, saying, I have need to be baptized of thee, and comest thou to me?[7] 15. And Jesus answering said unto him, Suffer it to be so now: for thus it becometh us to fulfil all righteousness. Then he suffered him. 16. And Jesus, when he was baptized, went up straightway out of the water: and, lo, the heavens were opened unto him,[8] and he saw the Spirit of God descending like a dove,[9] and lighting upon

---

[6] 13. *Then cometh Jesus from Galilee to Jordan unto John, to be baptized of him.* In *Against Pelagius* iii. 2.) Jerome states that the Gospel of the Hebrews has "The mother of the lord and his brothers said to him, 'John the Baptist baptizes for the forgiveness of sins; let us go and be baptized by him.' But he said to them, 'In what way have I sinned that I should go and be baptized by him? Unless, perhaps, what I have just said is a sin of ignorance.'"

[7] 14. *comest thou to me?* The question here is this: If Jesus were sinless, why did he need to be baptized for "remission of sins"?

[8] 16. *the heavens were opened unto him.* The words "unto him" are not in the earliest manuscripts of Matthew, such as Sinaiticus and Vaticanus.
    Omit *unto him*: א, B, sy^c, sy^s, sa
    to him: 𝕂, C, D, W, λ, φ, it, vg, sy^p, bo

[9] 16. *and he [Jesus] saw the Spirit of God descending like a dove.* This is where the Adoptionistic Gnostics, like the Ebionites, say that Jesus became "Christ." The "holy spirit" came out of heaven and descended on Jesus "like a dove." But only Jesus "saw" this vision. If he was the only one who witnessed it, then how did Matthew or anyone else find out about it unless Jesus himself revealed it?

him: 17. And lo a voice from heaven, saying, This is my beloved Son, in whom I am well pleased.[10]

(Cf. John 5:31, where Jesus says, "If I bear witness of myself, my witness is not true.")

[10] *17. This is my beloved son, in whom I am well pleased.* The terms often used in Christianity have quite different meanings in the original Hebrew; words such as "scripture," "Messiah," "salvation," and "Bible." What the phrase "son of God" meant to Jesus was different from what later Christians thought. First Chronicles 28:6 (God speaking to David) says, "Your son Solomon—he shall build My Temple and My courtyards; for I have chosen him to be a son for Me, and I will be a Father for him." There is certainly no connotation of divinity in this statement, and the phrase "son of God" is seen to be a term for the king of Israel, not a literal "son of God incarnate," as the Christians claim.

IV

1. Then was Jesus led up of the Spirit into the wilderness to be tempted of the devil.[1] *2. And when he had fasted forty days and forty nights, he was afterward an hungred. 3. And when the tempter came to him, he said, If thou be the Son of God, command that these stones be made bread. 4. But he answered and said, It is written, Man shall not live by bread alone,*[2] *but by every word that proceedeth out of the mouth of God. 5. Then the devil taketh him up into the holy city, and setteth him on a pinnacle of the temple, 6. And saith unto him, If thou be the Son of God, cast thyself down: for it is written, He shall give his angels charge concerning thee: and in their hands they shall bear thee up, lest at any time thou dash thy foot against a stone. 7. Jesus said unto him, It is written again, Thou shalt not tempt the Lord thy God.*[3] *8. Again, the devil*

---

[1] 4:1. *Then was Jesus led up of the Spirit into the wilderness to be tempted of the devil.* Where did the author of Matthew get this information? Again, only Jesus would have known about this incident. This whole passage about Jesus being tempted by Satan is most likely a fabrication, either by Jesus himself or by the writer of Matthew to (again) draw comparisons with the forty days Moses spent on Mount Sinai.

[2] 4. *Man shall not live by bread alone.* The Hebrew word לחם (*lechem*) has two primary meanings: "bread" and "to wage war" (plus, on rare occasions, "woman", *Rashi, Bereishis* 39:6). "'Bread' is the nourishment that man wrests from nature, in competition with his fellow men ... the joint product of nature and of the intelligence with which man masters the world" (Rabbi S. R. Hirsch, commentary to Deut. 8:3).

[3] 7. *Thou shalt not tempt the Lord thy God.* Deuteronomy 6:16: "You shall not test *HaShem*, your God, as you tested Him at Massah." The Torah teaches that we should not base our faith on miracles. In *Parashas Vayishlach*, Jacob does everything he can to appease Esau's wrath, taking precautions and even sending Esau gifts. Even if we have complete faith in God to protect us, we must do everything we can to prevent misfortune and to not rely on miracles. Also, the Torah makes it clear that God will send false prophets to do signs and wonders in order to test us: "If there should stand up in your midst a prophet or a dreamer of a dream, and he will produce to you a sign or a wonder, and the sign or the wonder comes about, of which he spoke to you, saying, 'Let us follow gods of others that you did not know and we shall worship them!'—do not hearken to the words of that prophet or to that dreamer of a dream, for *HaShem*, your God, is testing you to know whether you love *HaShem*, your God, with all your heart

taketh him up into an exceeding high mountain,[4] *and sheweth him all the kingdoms of the world, and the glory of them; 9. And saith unto him, All these things will I give thee, if thou wilt fall down and worship me. 10. Then saith Jesus unto him, Get thee hence, Satan: for it is written, Thou shalt worship the Lord thy God,*[5] *and Him only shalt thou serve. 11. Then the devil leaveth him, and, behold, angels came and ministered unto him. 12. Now when Jesus had heard that John was cast into prison, he departed into Galilee; 13. And leaving Nazareth, he came and dwelt in Capernaum, which is upon the sea coast, in the borders of Zabulon and Nephthalim: 14. That it might be fulfilled which was spoken by Esaias the prophet, saying, 15. The land of Zabulon,*[6] *and the land of Nephthalim, by*

---

and with all your soul. *HaShem*, your God, shall you follow and Him shall you fear; His commandments shall you observe and to His voice shall you hearken; Him shall you serve and to Him shall you cleave" (Deuteronomy 13:2–5). Our faith should be in God and not on the acts of a "miracle-worker." Christianity, which indeed bases its faith on the many "miracles" of Jesus, violates this very teaching.

[4] 8. *Again, the devil taketh him up into an exceeding high mountain.* In Matthew 4:8 from the Gospel according to the Hebrews (in Origen, *Commentary on John* 2:12 and *Homily on Jeremiah* 15:4): "And if any accept the Gospel of the Hebrews, here the Savior says: 'Even so did my mother, the Holy Spirit, take me by one of my hairs and carry me to the great Mount Tabor.'" The Holy Spirit is, in Gnostic terminology, Sophia, the mother of the Demiurge. Jerome also records these words in Latin in his commentaries on Micah 7:6, Isaiah 40:9 ff., and Ezekiel 16:13.

[5] 10. *Thou shalt worship the Lord thy God.* The text of the Torah says, "*HaShem*, your God, you shall fear" Deuteronomy 6:13). The Torah teaches us that we should both love and fear God. "Fear" means to hold God in awe and regard Him with great respect, as the awe we would feel in the presence of someone of great power and authority, such as a king or a president.

[6] 15. *The land of Zabulon.* Once again, we must look at the entire verse in the *Tanach* to put this in its proper perspective: "For he was not wearied the first time (the land) was distressed, when (Assyria) exiled the land of Zebulun and the land of Naphtali, but the last time (Assyria) will be severe, by the way of the sea, beyond the Jordan, the region of the nations. The people that walked in darkness have seen a great light; those who dwelled in the land of the shadow of death, light has shone upon them" (Isaiah 8:23–9:1). This was a prophecy about Sennacherib, not Jesus. This Gnostic interpretation of the Hebrew Scriptures is an interpretation that goes against the context of the passage.

the way of the sea, beyond Jordan, Galilee of the Gentiles; 16. The people which sat in darkness saw great light; and to them which sat in the region and shadow of death light is sprung up. 17. From that time Jesus began to preach, and to say, Repent: for the kingdom of heaven is at hand. 18. And Jesus, walking by the sea of Galilee, saw two brethren, Simon called Peter, and Andrew his brother, casting a net into the sea: for they were fishers. 19. And he saith unto them, Follow me, and I will make you fishers of men. 20. And they straightway left their nets, and followed him. 21. And going on from thence, he saw other two brethren, James the son of Zebedee, and John his brother, in a ship with Zebedee their father, mending their nets; and he called them. 22. And they immediately left the ship and their father, and followed him. 23. And Jesus went about all Galilee, teaching in their synagogues,[7] and preaching the gospel of the kingdom, and healing all manner of sickness and all manner of disease among the people. 24. And his fame went throughout all Syria: and they brought unto him all sick people that were taken with divers diseases and torments, and those which were possessed with devils, and those which were lunatick, and those that had the palsy; and he healed them. 25. And there followed him great multitudes of people from Galilee, and from Decapolis, and from Jerusalem, and from Judaea, and from beyond Jordan.

---

[7] *23. And Jesus went about all Galilee, teaching in their synagogues.* That is, the synagogues of the Jews.

V

1. And seeing the multitudes,[1] *he went up into*[2] *a mountain: and when he was set, his disciples came unto him: 2. And he opened his mouth, and taught them, saying,*[3] *3. Blessed are the poor in spirit:*

---

[1] 5:1. *And seeing the multitudes.* The multitudes that followed Jesus (cf. 4:25) were Jews, not gentiles (cf. 4:23). Again, there is nothing to suggest that Jesus was leading a gentile movement at any point in his ministry.

[2] 1. *he went up into a mountain.* Greek εἰς, "into." The status of Matthew as the most popular gospel rests in no small part on these three chapters (5, 6, 7), which are known as the Sermon on the Mount. The Sermon on the Mount is a simple and straightforward discourse, uncluttered with the supernatural miracle stories that were added later to entice the pagan gentiles into the church. This sermon contains the main body of Jesus's ethical teaching, and many of the most widely quoted passages from the New Testament come from this sermon, including the beatitudes ("Blessed are the poor in spirit: for theirs is the kingdom of heaven"), the similitudes ("Ye are the light of the world"), and his teachings on such subjects as life, prayer, money, and marriage. It is here that we find two of the most famous of all Jesus's teachings, the Golden Rule and the Lord's Prayer. If the New Testament is the foundation for Christianity, and the four gospels are the foundation of the New Testament, and Matthew's Sermon on the Mount is the foundation for the ethical teachings of Jesus, then the importance of the Sermon on the Mount to the religion of Christianity, the largest and most powerful organized religion in history, cannot be overstated.

Keeping this in mind, it should be pointed out, first, that the Sermon on the Mount is the most Jewish part of the most Jewish of gospels, and, second, the power of these three chapters comes not from Jesus himself, but from the Torah of Moses. Practically all of Jesus's sayings and teachings found in these three chapters are teachings that were taken straight out of rabbinic Judaism, from either the Tanach or the Oral Law. Much has been written about the "uniqueness" and "genius" of Jesus's teaching, starting with the author of Matthew himself (cf. Matt. 7:28–29), yet the "genius" of Jesus consists of his drawing on the vast repository of wisdom from other rabbis (the Pharisees), as found in the Oral Law, and passing it all off as his own teaching. Very little of the Sermon on the Mount is original; the only original parts are where Jesus teaches not only against established *halacha*, but outright violations of the Torah.

[3] 2. *and taught them, saying.* It is apparent from the context of the Sermon on the Mount that Jesus was speaking to a Jewish audience. His entire sermon deals with issues that are some of the major themes of the Torah, such as, in the Beatitudes, justice to the poor and downtrodden (cf. Exodus 22:25, 23:11, Leviticus 19:10, Deuteronomy 10:17–18, 14:28–29, 15:7–11, 24:19). Jesus also would give a *midrash* on a particular teaching, as well as his own personal rulings for

for theirs is the kingdom of heaven.[4] *4. Blessed are they that mourn: for they shall be comforted.*[5] *5. Blessed are the meek: for they shall inherit the earth.*[6] *6. Blessed are they which do hunger and thirst after righteousness: for they shall be filled.*[7] *7. Blessed are the merciful: for they shall obtain mercy.*[8] *8. Blessed are the pure in heart: for they shall see God.*[9] *9. Blessed are the peacemakers: for they shall be called the children of God.*[10] *10. Blessed are they which*

---

specific laws of the Torah (*halacha*), as in Deuteronomy 24:1. It is obvious that Jesus was familiar with the Oral Law (the Talmud), which the gospels call "the traditions of the elders."

[4] *3. Blessed are the poor in spirit: for theirs is the kingdom of heaven.* This concept is found in the *Tanach*: *[A] lowly spirit will support (his) honor* (Proverbs 29:23).

[5] *4. Blessed are they that mourn: for they shall be comforted.* Cf. *He is the Healer of the brokenhearted, and the One Who binds up their sorrows* (Psalm 147:3).

[6] *5. Blessed are the meek: for they shall inherit the earth.* Cf. *But the humble shall inherit the earth* (Psalm 37:11).

[7] *6. Blessed are they which do hunger and thirst after righteousness: for they shall be filled.* Cf. *When You will bless the righteous, HaShem, You will envelop him with favor like a shield* (Psalm 5:13). Rabban Shimon ben Gamliel says, "The world endures on three things; justice, truth, and peace, as it is said: Truth and the verdict of peace are you to adjudicate in your gates" (Zechariah 8:16, *Pirkei Avot* 1:18).

[8] *7. Blessed are the merciful: for they shall obtain mercy.* Rabbi Gamliel said, "Whoever has mercy upon creatures will be granted mercy from heaven" (*Shabbat* 151b). This is the same Rabbi Gamliel who is mentioned in the New Testament (Acts 5:34, 22:3). Rabbi Gamliel was the grandson of the famous Rabbi Hillel, who died when Jesus was a child. Many of the rabbis who are quoted in the Talmud were contemporary with Jesus, though some were earlier, some, later. It must be kept in mind, however, that the oral tradition that they (as well as Jesus) quoted from was ancient. It was handed down in an unbroken line of teachers going back to Moses (cf. *Pirkei Avot* 1:1).

[9] *8. Blessed are the pure in heart: for they shall see God.* Cf. *Who may ascend the mountain of HaShem, and who may stand in the place of His sanctity? One with clean hands and pure heart"* (Psalms 24:3–4).

[10] *9. Blessed are the peacemakers: for they shall be called the children of God.* "Hillel says: 'Be among the disciples of Aaron, loving peace and pursuing peace, loving people, and bringing them closer to the Torah.'" (*Pirkei Avot* 1:12) In contrast to this, one of the fundamental principles of Christian theology is to

are persecuted for righteousness' sake: for theirs is the kingdom of heaven.[11] *11. Blessed are ye, when men shall revile you, and persecute you, and shall say all manner of evil against you falsely, for my sake.*[12] *12. Rejoice, and be exceeding glad: for great is your reward in heaven: for so persecuted they the prophets which were before you. 13. Ye are the salt of the earth: but if the salt have lost his savour, wherewith shall it be salted? it is thenceforth good for nothing, but to be cast out, and to be trodden under foot of men. 14. Ye are the light of the world.*[13] *A city that is set on an hill cannot be hid.*[14] *15. Neither do men light a candle, and put it under a bushel, but on a candlestick; and it giveth light unto all that are in the house. 16. Let your light so shine before men, that they may see your good works,*[15] *and glorify your Father which is in heaven.*[16]

---

turn people away from the Torah.

[11] 10. *Blessed are they which are persecuted for righteousness' sake: for theirs is the kingdom of heaven.* "Rabbi Abbahu said, 'A man should always try to be among the persecuted rather than the persecutors'" (*Bava Kamma* 93a).

[12] 11. *Blessed are ye, when men shall revile you, and persecute you, and shall say all manner of evil against you falsely, for my sake.* The words ψευ όμενοι ("falsely") are absent in the early Western texts. It should also be pointed out that countless Jews over the centuries have been martyred in the "name" of Jesus.

[13] 14. *Ye are the light of the world.* In Judaism, one of the most important themes in the scriptures is that of the Jews being the keepers and bearers of the light of the Torah. God chose the Jews to be the teachers of mankind, to keep and protect the Torah throughout the ages. Christianity has always taught that this special status ended when the Jews "rejected" Jesus. The theme of the Jews being the bearers of the heavenly light that was in the Torah is a theme that runs throughout the Bible (cf. Exodus 19:5–6, Deuteronomy 7:6–9, Isaiah 41:8–13, 42:1–9, 43:8–11, 49:1–6, 51:4–8, Zechariah 8:22–23). This theme must be kept in mind when reading the *Tanach* and, certainly, the New Testament.

[14] 14. *A city that is set on an hill.* Cf. "Jesus says, 'A city built on the top of a high mountain and established can neither fall nor be hidden'" (Oxyrhynchus Papyrus 1, Logion 7). "A city built on a high mountain and fortified can neither fall nor be hidden" (Gospel of Thomas, Logion 32).

[15] 16. *that they may see your good works.* Obviously, the works of the Law.

[16] 16. *and glorify your Father which is in heaven.* The example of the Jewish people, by keeping the Torah, will eventually win over the nations to the truth of God's Law.

17. Think not that I am come to destroy the law, or the prophets: I am not come to destroy, but to fulfil.[17] *18. For verily*[18] *I say unto you, Till heaven and earth pass, one jot or one tittle shall in no wise pass from the law,*[19] *till all be fulfilled. 19. Whosoever*

---

[17] 17. *Think not that I am come to destroy the law.* Matthew 5:17 is perhaps the most misunderstood and misinterpreted verse in the entire New Testament. According to Christian theology, Jesus did not destroy the Law; he "fulfilled" it for everyone thereafter by keeping it perfectly. There are many problems with this interpretation, not the least of which is the word "fulfill", πληρῶσαι in the Greek, which means to "perform" or "accomplish." This is the same exact word used in Matthew 3:15, when Jesus tells John the Baptist that he must "perform" the commandment of the *mikvah*, which is where the Christian concept of "baptism" comes from. If Jesus had "fulfilled" the concept of baptizing, why then do Christians continue to do it? (cf. commentary to Matthew 28:19).

In his *Against Heresies* xxx.16:5, Epiphanius claims that the Gospel of the Ebionites states this verse as "I have come to destroy sacrifices; and if you do not stop making sacrifices, the wrath (of God) will not leave you." Clement of Alexandria wrote (in *Miscellanies* iii.9:63) that the Gospel of the Egyptians has "I have come to destroy the works of the female." This is possibly a reference to Sophia, who according to the Gnostics was the archon who gave birth to the Demiurge. It is also worth noting that this verse is the only quote from Jesus in the Talmud: "I come not to destroy the Law of Moses, nor to add to the Law of Moses" (*Shabbat* 116b). Although much of what the Talmud says about Jesus of Nazareth is uncomplimentary, it should be noted that this one solitary teaching says that Jesus did not come to either add to or take away from the Torah. Since so many of Jesus's teachings are problematic (not to mention how problematic is the massive editing and rephrasing of Jesus's own words by later "correctors") and the teachings of Jesus that agreed with the other rabbis could be found elsewhere in the *Tanach* and the Talmud, it makes little sense to study Jesus's teachings in order to learn Torah, particularly when we have to scrape away the centuries of Gnostic theological interpretations that have encrusted themselves to his sayings. To discern which teachings of Jesus are halachically viable, we must know a good deal of Torah already, which makes the study of the New Testament and its small amount of Torah quotations an exercise in futility. If we are thirsty, why drink from the muddied and fouled puddle when there is a cool, clear spring right next to it?

[18] 18. *For verily.* The Greek word ἀμὴν, from the Hebrew אמן (*ahmein*, usually translated as "amen"), is used to punctuate or confirm a teaching or a saying that immediately precedes it. In Christian translations, it is given as either "truly" or "verily" and incorrectly connected with the sentence following it.

[19] 18. *law.* Cf. Deuteronomy 4:2. There is a paper by Doron Witztum, Eliyaho Rips, and Yoav Rosenburg on the secret codes found in the Book of Genesis in

therefore shall break one of these least commandments,[20] *and shall teach men so, he shall be called the least in the kingdom of heaven: but whosoever shall do and teach them, the same shall be called great in the kingdom of heaven.*[21] *20. For I say unto you, That*

---

the August, 1994, edition of the scholarly journal *Statistical Science* from the Institute of Mathematical Statistics (Vol. 9, no. 3, 429–438). These three authors discovered that when the Hebrew letters of Genesis were lined up in rows and subjected to a computer program that searched for equidistant letter sequences, many names, dates, and messages would appear, too many to be a mere coincidence. Their conclusion is that the Torah is like a tremendously complex computer program with an unbelievable amount of information hidden within its text. This reinforces what the rabbis have been teaching for centuries: that the Torah contained an enormous amount of information to those who could unlock its secrets. This is why the Jews have, over millennia, taken scrupulous care in copying down the Torah so that all Torah scrolls are the same. This is different from the treatment of the text of the New Testament, which was edited extensively throughout the centuries. Jesus also teaches this important principle, that not one letter of the Torah is ever to be altered, which was the opposite approach to the actual treatment of the New Testament, where there are hundreds of thousands of textual differences in the five thousand or so Greek manuscripts.

[20] 19. *Whosoever therefore shall break one of these least commandments.* Rabbi (Yehuhdah HaNasi) said: "Be as scrupulous in performing a 'minor' mitzvah (commandment) as in a 'major' one" (*Pirkei Avot* 2:1).

[21] 19. *the kingdom of heaven.* Because it negates the teaching of Jesus's "fulfilling" the Law, this verse has been one of the most difficult verses in the New Testament for Christian theologians to explain. To grasp this verse in its proper perspective, we must turn to the Torah: Deuteronomy 13:1–6 (Deuteronomy 12:32–13:5 in the Christian Bible) and Deuteronomy 18:15–22. We start with Deuteronomy13:1 (Deuteronomy 12:32 in the Christian Bibles): "Everything that I command you, you shall carry out punctiliously; you must not add anything to it nor subtract anything from it" (Hirsch). This verse alone poses major problems for Christianity, since so many of Jesus's teachings were altered.

The next five verses (Deuteronomy 13:2–6) say, *If there should stand up in your midst a prophet or a dreamer of a dream, and he will produce to you a sign or a wonder, and the sign or the wonder comes about, of which he spoke to you, saying, 'Let us follow gods of others that you did not know and we shall worship them!'—do not hearken to the words of that prophet or to that dreamer of a dream, for HaShem, your God, is testing you to know whether you love HaShem, your God, will all your heart and with all your soul. HaShem, your God, shall you follow and Him shall you fear; His commandments shall you observe and to His voice shall you hearken; Him shall you serve and to Him shall you cleave. And that prophet and that dreamer of a dream shall be put to death, for he had spoken perversion against HaShem, your God.* This reinforces what is mentioned in the footnote for the previous verse, that nothing in the Torah is to be changed. What this teaches is that if a prophet arises who tries to lead Israel away from God, this teaching transgresses the Torah and he is a false prophet who should be put to death. God himself warns Israel that a false prophet is a test to see if the Jews will keep the Torah.

Deuteronomy 18:18–22 says, *I will raise up for them (Israel) a prophet from among their (own) brethren, like yourself, and I will put My words into his mouth, so that he may speak to them everything that I will command him. And it shall be that the man who will not hearken to My words that he will speak in My Name, of him will I demand (an accounting). But a prophet who will speak wantonly in My Name a word that I did not command him to speak, or one who will speak in the name of other gods, that prophet shall die. And if you will then say in your heart, 'How can we recognize the word that God has not spoken?'—That which the prophet speaks in the name of God, and the word does not materialize and does not come (true), that is the word God has not spoken; the prophet has spoken it wantonly. You shall not be afraid of him* (Hirsch). What we have here is how the Jews were able to distinguish between a false prophet and a true prophet in the cases where the prophet is not trying to lead Israel away from the Torah.

This has serious implications for Christianity. First of all, the theological teaching was that Jesus "fulfilled" the Law and in doing so changed the Law so that neither Jew nor gentile had to keep the laws of the Torah anymore. Nowhere in the Torah does it say that the laws and commandments that God gave to Israel would be done away with at a later date when he sent his "son" to "fulfill" them. Instead, over and over, God hammers in the idea that the laws of the Torah are permanent and to be observed for all time (cf. Exodus 12:14, 12:17, 12:24, 19:9, 29:9, 29:28, 31:13–17, Leviticus 3:17, 7:36, 16:29–34, 23:21, 23:31, Numbers 10:8, 15:15).

In light of the two passages from Deuteronomy, we see that God told the Jews that if a prophet, or someone who could perform miracles, tried to change any of the laws of the Torah and teach other Jews to do so, this man is a false prophet. God had told them to be on the lookout for such a person, for He was testing them to see if they would keep His Law. Furthermore, if such a false prophet arose, he should be put to death for trying to lead the children of Israel astray. Deuteronomy 18 also teaches that a true prophet is required to show a "sign" or "wonder" to prove that he is, indeed, a true prophet. In *Hilchot Yesodei HaTorah* 10:1, Maimonides explains that "the sign of [the truth of his prophecy] will be the fulfillment of his prediction of future events ... should even a minute particular of his 'prophecy' not materialize, he is surely a false prophet" (cf. commentary below to Matthew 12:39–40, 16:28, and 24:34). If the Christian say is true, therefore, that Jesus did claim to "fulfill" the Law, then he is a false

except your righteousness shall exceed the righteousness of the scribes and Pharisees,[22] ye shall in no case enter into the kingdom of heaven. 21. Ye have heard that it was said by them of old time, Thou shalt not kill; and whosoever shall kill shall be in danger of the judgment: 22. But I say unto you, That whosoever is angry with his brother without a cause[23] shall be in danger of the judgment: and whosoever shall say to his brother, Raca,[24] shall be in danger of the council: but whosoever shall say, Thou fool,[25] shall be in danger of hell[26] fire. 23. Therefore if thou bring thy gift to the altar, and there rememberest that thy brother hath ought against thee; 24. Leave there thy gift before the altar, and go thy way; first be reconciled to thy brother, and then come and offer thy gift. 25.

---

prophet under the law of the Torah, and the Jews were correct in not only not following him, but also, in total accordance with God's command, they would have been correct in having him sentenced to death. Ironically, not to have sentenced Jesus to death would have made the Jews guilty of violating the Law.

[22] 20. *the scribes and the Pharisees.* Jesus exhorts the Jews to be even more scrupulous in keeping the Law than the scribes and the Pharisees. Much is made in Christian theology about his teaching concerning "going beyond the letter of the Law," and yet the Talmud teaches the exact same thing: "The Jewish state fell because its inhabitants were content to act simply in accordance with the strict letter of the Law" (*Bava Metzia* 30b). The Law is a bare minimum of what we must do; it is the starting place, not the end.

[23] 22. *angry with his brother without a cause.* Hillel said, "Do not judge your fellow until you have reached his place" (*Pirkei Avot* 2:5). This verse has also been altered as follows:
　　with his brother without a cause (𝕶, D, W, Θ, λ, φ, it, sy^c, sy^s, sy^p, sa, bo)
　　angry with a brother or sister (omit without a cause): (𝔭^{67}?, ℵ, B, vg, Justin, Origen).

[24] 22. *Raca.* Rabbi Elazar the Moda'ite said, "One who ... humiliates his fellow in public ... has no share in the World to Come" (*Pirkei Avot* 3:15).

[25] 22. *Thou fool.* Cf. Matthew 23:17, where Jesus himself breaks his own "rule": *Ye fools, and blind! for whether is greater, the gold, or the temple that sanctifieth the gold?*

[26] 22. *hell.* Yehudah ben Tema said, "The brazen goes to Gehinnon, but the shamefaced goes to the Garden of Eden." (*Pirkei Avot* 5:24). To the south of Jerusalem is the valley of Gehinnon, where the citizens of Jerusalem burned their refuse. It was usually smoking from the fires.

Agree with thine adversary quickly, whiles thou art in the way with him; lest at any time the adversary deliver thee to the judge, and the judge deliver thee to the officer, and thou be cast into prison. 26. Verily I say unto thee, Thou shalt by no means come out thence, till thou hast paid the uttermost farthing. 27. Ye have heard that it was said by them of old time, Thou shalt not commit adultery: 28. But I say unto you, That whosoever looketh on a woman to lust after her hath committed adultery[27] *with her already in his heart.*[28] *29. And if thy right eye offend thee,*[29] *pluck it out,*[30] *and cast it from thee: for it is profitable for thee that one of thy members should perish, and not that thy whole body should be cast into hell. 30. And if thy right hand offend thee, cut it off, and cast it from thee: for it is profitable for thee that one of thy members should perish, and not that thy whole body should be cast into hell. 31. It hath been said, Whosoever shall put away his wife, let him give her a writing of divorcement: 32. But I say unto you, That whosoever shall put away his wife, saving for the cause of fornication, causeth her to commit adultery: and whosoever shall marry her that is divorced committeth adultery. 33. Again, ye have heard that it hath been said by them of old time, Thou shalt not forswear thyself, but shalt perform unto the Lord thine oaths: 34. But I say unto you, Swear not at all; neither by heaven; for it is God's throne: 35. Nor by the earth; for it is his footstool: neither by Jerusalem; for it is the city of the great King. 36. Neither shalt thou swear by thy head,*

---

[27] 28. *adultery.* The Sages said, "Anyone who converses excessively with a woman causes evil to himself, neglects Torah study and will eventually inherit Gehinnon" (*Pirkei Avot* 1:5).

[28] 28. *whosoever looketh on a woman to lust after her hath committed adultery with her already in his heart.* Cf. "He who regards a woman with an impure intention is as if he had already had relations with her" (*Kallah*, chapter 1).

[29] 29. *And if thy right eye offend thee.* Cf. Rabbi Yochanan ben Zakkai, who said, "Go out and discern which is the evil path from which a man should distance himself." Rabbi Eliezer said, "An evil eye" (*Pirkei Avot* 2:14). Rabbi Yehoshua said, "An evil eye, the evil inclination, and hatred of other people remove a person from the world" (*Pirkei Avot* 2:16).

[30] 29. *pluck it out.* Leviticus 19:28 remarks on the pagan practice of self-mutilation for grieving for the dead. Self-mutilation in any form or for any reason is a violation of Torah (*Makkot* 21a; cf. Deut. 14:1, Lev. 19:27–28, 21:5).

because thou canst not make one hair white or black. 37. But let your communication be, Yea, yea; Nay, nay:[31] *for whatsoever is more than these cometh of evil. 38. Ye have heard that it hath been said, An eye for an eye,*[32] *and a tooth for a tooth: 39. But I say unto you, That ye resist not evil: but whosoever shall smite thee on thy right cheek, turn to him the other also.*[33] *40. And if any man will sue thee at the law, and take away thy coat, let him have thy cloak also.*[34] *41. And whosoever shall compel thee to go a mile, go with him twain. 42. Give to him that asketh thee, and from him that would borrow of thee turn not thou away. 43. Ye have heard that it hath been said, Thou shalt love thy neighbour, and hate thine enemy.*[35] *44. But I say unto you, Love your enemies, bless them that curse you, do good to them that hate you, and pray for them which despitefully use you, and persecute you;*[36] *45. That ye may be the children of your Father which is in heaven: for he maketh his sun to rise on the evil and on the good,*[37] *and sendeth rain on the just*

---

[31] 37. *But let your communication be, Yea, yea; Nay, nay.* Rabbi Judah said, "your 'Yes' shall be true, and your 'No' shall be true" (*Bava Metzia* 49a).

[32] 38. *An eye for an eye.* What if a man with one eye puts out one eye of a man that has two eyes? Does this mean that the one-eyed man is to be blinded? The Talmud (*Bava Kamma* 83b) explains that the verse from Exodus 21:24 is not meant literally, but has to do with monetary compensation.

[33] 39. *turn to him the other also.* Cf. *Let one offer his cheek to his smiter* (Lamentations 3:30).

[34] 40. *let him have thy cloak also.* "[Noahides] are obligated to observe a system of civil law based on returning either the exact amount owed to its rightful owner or arranging a suitable compromise … there is no basis in the Noahide system to penalize a person to pay more than the normal compensation" (*Talmud Bavli, Sanhedrin* 56b³, vol. 2, Schottenstein Edition, Brooklyn: Mesorah Publications, Ltd., 2005).

[35] 43. *and hate thine enemy.* The dictum of "hating one's enemy" is certainly not in Leviticus 19:18, nor is it implied. This is a clear case of Jesus adding to the text of the Torah.

[36] 44. *and pray for them which despitefully use you, and persecute you.* Cf. Proverbs 25:21: *If your foe is hungry, feed him bread; and if he is thirsty, give him water to drink.*

[37] 45. *the evil and on the good.* Shmuel HaKattan said, "When your enemy falls be not glad, and when he stumbles let your heart not be joyous" (*Pirkei Avot*

and on the unjust. 46. For if ye love them which love you, what reward have ye? do not even the publicans the same? 47. And if ye salute your brethren only, what do ye more than others? do not even the publicans so?[38] *48. Be ye therefore perfect, even as your Father which is in heaven is perfect.*[39]

4:24).

[38] 47. *do not even the publicans so?* Cf. ἐθνικō (do not even the gentiles so?) Here Jesus is using the gentiles as an example of sinful behavior. It is obvious from the context that the crowd he is speaking to is composed of Jews.

[39] 48. *Be ye therefore perfect, even as your Father which is in heaven is perfect.* Abba Saul said, "Be like Him … just as He is gracious and compassionate, so you be gracious and compassionate" (*Shabbat* 133b).

VI

1. Take heed that ye do not your alms before men,[1] *to be seen of them: otherwise ye have no reward of your Father which is in heaven. 2. Therefore when thou doest thine alms, do not sound a trumpet before thee, as the hypocrites do in the synagogues and in the streets, that they may have glory of men. Verily I say unto you, they have their reward. 3. But when thou doest alms,*[2] *let not thy left hand know what thy right hand doeth:*[3] *4. That thine alms may be in secret: and thy Father which seeth in secret himself shall reward thee openly.*[4] *5. And when thou prayest, thou shalt not be as the hypocrites are: for they love to pray standing in the synagogues and in the corners of the streets, that they may be seen of men. Verily I say unto you, they have their reward. 6. But thou, when thou prayest, enter into thy closet, and when thou hast shut thy door, pray to thy Father which is in secret; and thy Father which seeth in secret shall reward thee openly.*[5] *7. But*

---

[1] 6:1. *Take heed that ye do not your alms before men.* Early Greek texts, including Sinaticus, Vaticanus, and Beaze, have *Beware of practicing your piety before others* (א, B, D, λ, it, vg, sy^s, sy^p). Other texts have *Beware of giving your alms before others* (𝕂, W, Θ, φ).

[2] 3. *But when thou doest alms.* It is instructive to know the Hebrew language to understand the link between justice and charity. There are three words based on the Hebrew root צדק: צדק, "justice," צדיק, "a righteous person," and צדקה, "charity."

[3] 3. *let not thy left hand know what thy right hand doeth.* Rabbi Eleazar said, "A man who gives charity in secret is greater" (*Bava Bathra* 9b).

[4] 4. *which seeth in secret himself shall reward thee openly.* Sinaticus, Vaticanus, and Bezae (and many other early texts) have *who sees in secret will reward you.* Other texts add "openly."

    who sees in secret will reward you: א, B, D, λ, φ, it (some MSS.), vg, sy^c, sa, bo
    Add "openly": 𝕂, W, Θ, it (some MSS.), sy^s, sy$^{p.}$

[5] 6. *and thy Father which seeth in secret shall reward thee openly.* Another corrupted text:

    who sees in secret will reward you: א, B, D, λ, φ, it (some MSS.), vg, sy^c, sy^s, sa, bo
    Add "openly": 𝕂, W, Θ, it (some MSS.), sy^p

when ye pray, use not vain repetitions, as the heathen do:[6] *for they think that they shall be heard for their much speaking.*[7] *8. Be not ye therefore like unto them: for your Father knoweth what things ye have need of, before ye ask him.*[8] *9. After this manner*

---

[6] 7. *But when ye pray, use not vain repetitions, as the heathen do.* The Greek word for "heathen" is ἐθνικō or "gentiles." Again, Jesus uses gentile behavior as an example of sinful behavior. He had little regard for gentiles, calling them "dogs" and "heathens" and "swine" (cf. Matthew 7:6, 15:26).

[7] 7. *for they think that they shall be heard for their much speaking.* Rabbi Shammai said, "Say little and do much" (*Pirkei Avot* 1:15). "Rabbi Huna said in the name of Rabbi Meir; 'A man's words should always be few in addressing God'" (*Berakoth* 61a).

[8] 8. *your Father knoweth what things ye have need of, before ye ask him.* It is important for the Noahide to understand the Jewish concept of prayer. Prayer should not be viewed as simply meditation or supplication. Rabbi S. R. Hirsch explains, "להתפלל means to perform this task upon one's own person. התפלל means: *Take the element of God's truth and allow it to penetrate every aspect and relationship of our character, thus attaining for ourselves that harmonious integrity of all of life which can be gained only through God.* Consequently, Jewish תפלה is diametrically opposed to what is generally described as 'prayer.' It is not an outpouring from within, an expression of things with which the heart is already replete ... rather, it implies an absorption and penetration of truths which come from outside oneself ... a labor upon one's own inner self to elevate it to that level at which it can perceive the truth and make decisions in keeping with the will of God" (Hirsch, *T'rumath Tzvi*, 99).

Because prayer and the other forms of the Jewish service of God are not included in the Seven Laws, prayer and worship should be an individual choice for the Noahide. The basic framework of the Noahide Law as taught in the Oral Law gives the Noahide the extraordinary freedom to pray as he or she pleases. Noahides can certainly use a Noahide Siddur if they so wish. They can also use the psalms or even devise their own personal prayers. It is all a matter of personal choice. Noahides who desire "group prayer" should center this activity on the family, the fundamental building block of a healthy Torah-based society. What is important is that the Noahide must realize that prayer is a means to an end, not simply an end to itself. Noahides who observe the "religious" elements of the Torah that were given specifically to the Jews—praying from a Noahide siddur while wearing a talis, keeping Sukkot, putting up a mezuzah on their doorpost, and so on—are taking upon themselves the commandments that were given to Israel to remind them of their mission. Israel's duty to God is a full-time job, particularly when they are out in the secular world doing business. The Noahide who ignores the basic laws of theft and social justice will be in for a rude shock when he is judged in the heavenly court. A Noahide should view

therefore pray ye:[9] *Our Father which art in heaven, Hallowed be thy name. 10. Thy kingdom come. Thy will be done in earth, as it is in heaven. 11. Give us this day our daily bread. 12. And forgive us our debts, as we forgive our debtors. 13. And lead us not into temptation, but deliver us from evil: For thine is the kingdom, and the power, and the glory, for ever. Amen.*[10] *14. For if ye forgive*

---

prayer as a spiritual strengthening, something to gird himself with God's truth as he goes out into the world to become a champion of צדק, "justice." Social justice is one of the Seven Laws of Noah.

[9] 9. *After this manner therefore pray ye.* This prayer is modeled on ancient and traditional rabbinic prayers, the *Shemoneh Esrei* and the Rabbi's *Kaddish*:

> *Our Father* [Bring us back, our Father, to Your Torah—*Shemoneh Esrei*]
>
> *which art in heaven* [We shall sanctify Your Name in this world, just as they sanctify it in heaven above—*Shemoneh Esrei*]
>
> *Hallowed be thy name* [May His great Name grow exalted and sanctified—Rabbi's *Kaddish*]
>
> *Thy kingdom come* [May He give reign to His kingship in your lifetimes and in your days, and in the lifetimes of the entire Family of Israel, swiftly and soon—Rabbi's *Kaddish*]
>
> *Thy will be done* [in the world that He created as He willed—Rabbi's *Kaddish*]
>
> *in earth, as it is in heaven.* [From before their Father Who is in Heaven (and on earth)—Rabbi's *Kaddish*]
>
> *Give us this day our daily bread* [Upon Israel, upon the teachers...ample nourishment—Rabbi's *Kaddish*]
>
> *And forgive us our debts, as we forgive our debtors* [Forgive us, our Father, for we have erred; pardon us, our King, for we have willfully sinned—*Shemoneh Esrei*]
>
> *And lead us not into temptation, but deliver us from evil*: [Endow us graciously from Yourself with wisdom, insight, and discernment—*Shemoneh Esrei*]
>
> *For thine is the kingdom, and the power, and the glory, for ever.* [From generation to generation we shall relate Your greatness and for infinite eternities we shall proclaim Your holiness. Your praise, our God, shall not leave our mouth forever and ever—*Shemoneh Esrei*].

[10] 13. *And lead us not into temptation, but deliver us from evil: For thine is the kingdom, and the power, and the glory, for ever. Amen.* Not even the most famous prayer in the New Testament, the Lord's Prayer, was safe from the hands of the Christian "correctors." The line "For thine is the kingdom, and the power,

men their trespasses, your heavenly Father will also forgive you: 15. But if ye forgive not men their trespasses, neither will your Father forgive your trespasses.[11] *16. Moreover when ye fast,*[12] *be not, as the hypocrites, of a sad countenance: for they disfigure their faces, that they may appear unto men to fast. Verily I say unto you, they have their reward. 17. But thou, when thou fastest, anoint thine head, and wash thy face; 18. That thou appear not unto men to fast, but unto thy Father which is in secret: and thy Father, which seeth in secret, shall reward thee openly. 19. Lay not up for yourselves treasures upon earth,*[13] *where moth and rust doth corrupt, and where thieves break through and steal: 20. But lay up for yourselves treasures in heaven, where neither moth nor rust doth corrupt, and where thieves do not break through nor steal:*[14]

---

and the glory, for ever. Amen" is not found in the oldest manuscripts.
    Omit entire verse: *For thine is the kingdom, and the power, and the glory, for ever. Amen*: ℵ, B, D, λ, it, vg, bo
    Include *For the kingdom and the power and the glory are yours forever. Amen*: 𝕂, W, Θ, φ, sy^p
    Include *For the power and the glory are yours forever. Amen*: sa (Didache: omit: *Amen*)
    Include *For the kingdom and the glory are yours forever. Amen* sy^c

[11] 15. *But if ye forgive not men their trespasses.* Cf. "Whose sin does He forgive? He who forgives transgression" (*Rosh Hashanah* 17a). This verse was also corrupted; early manuscripts, including Sinaiticus and Beaze as well as Augustine omit "their trespasses":
    Omit *their trespasses*: ℵ, D, λ, it, vg, sy^p, bo (some MSS.), Augustine.
    Include *others their trespasses*: 𝕂, B, W, Θ, φ, sy^c, sa, bo (some MSS.).

[12] 16. *Moreover when ye fast.* One early manuscript has "Jesus says, 'If you do not fast to the world, you will not find the kingdom of God, and if you do not keep the sabbath, you will not see the Father'" (Oxyrhynchus Papyrus 1, Logion 2). Another very early manuscript has "Do not let your fasts be with the hypocrites, for they fast on Mondays and Thursdays. But you are to fast on Wednesdays and Fridays" (Didache 8:1). Needless to say, fasting is not included in the Noahide Laws.

[13] 19. *Lay not up for yourselves treasures upon earth.* Hillel said, "The more possessions, the more worry" (*Pirkei Avot* 2:8).

[14] 20. *where thieves do not break through nor steal.* Cf. "After King Monbas'

21. For where your treasure is, there will your heart be also. 22. The light of the body is the eye: if therefore thine eye be single, thy whole body shall be full of light. 23. But if thine eye be evil, thy whole body shall be full of darkness. If therefore the light that is in thee be darkness, how great is that darkness! 24. No man can serve two masters: for either he will hate the one, and love the other; or else he will hold to the one, and despise the other. Ye cannot serve God and mammon.[15] *25. Therefore I say unto you, Take no thought for your life, what ye shall eat, or what ye shall drink;*[16] *nor yet for your body, what ye shall put on. Is not the life more than meat, and the body than raiment? 26. Behold the fowls of the air: for they sow not, neither do they reap, nor gather into barns; yet your heavenly Father feedeth them.*[17] *Are ye not much better than they? 27. Which of you by taking thought can add one cubit unto his stature? 28. And why take ye thought for raiment? Consider the lilies of the*

---

family rebuked him for giving away all the family's treasures, he answered: 'My ancestors stored treasures in a secret place that could be reached by human hands, but I have stored (them) in a place that can reached by no human hand'" (*Bava Bathra* 11a).

[15] 24. *Ye cannot serve God and mammon.* Rabbi Meir said, "Reduce your business activities and engage in Torah study" (*Pirkei Avot* 4:12).

[16] 25. *what ye shall eat, or what ye shall drink.* As with so many of Jesus's teachings, this passage shows the variation brought through oral transmission. Even two texts that are in the same family, such as Sinaiticus and Vaticanus, have differences; with certain early texts have *what you will eat or what you will drink*, or *what you shall eat and what you shall drink*, while some omit *or what ye shall drink*. One very early text, Oxyrhynchus Papyrus 655, has "(Take no thought) from morning until evening or from evening until morning, either for your food, what you will eat, or for your clothing, what you will wear. You are far better than the lilies which grow but do not spin. Having one piece of clothing, what do you (lack)? ... Who could add to your span of life? God will give you your clothing."

what you will eat or what you will drink: B, W, φ, it (some MSS.), sa (some MSS.), bo
what you shall eat and what you shall drink: K, Θ, sy^p
Omit *or what ye shall drink*: ℵ, λ, it (some MSS.), vg, sy^c, and sa (some MSS.).

[17] 26. *yet your heavenly Father feedeth them.* Cf. Psalm 147:9: He gives to an animal its food, to young ravens that cry out.

field, how they grow; they toil not, neither do they spin: 29. And yet I say unto you, that even Solomon in all his glory was not arrayed like one of these. 30. Wherefore, if God so clothe the grass of the field, which to day is, and to morrow is cast into the oven, shall he not much more clothe you, O ye of little faith? 31. Therefore take no thought, saying, What shall we eat? or, What shall we drink? or, Wherewithal shall we be clothed? 32. (For after all these things do the Gentiles seek:)[18] for your heavenly Father knoweth that ye have need of all these things. 33. But seek ye first the kingdom of God, and his righteousness; and all these things shall be added unto you.[19] 34. Take therefore no thought for the morrow: for the morrow shall take thought for the things of itself.[20] Sufficient unto the day is the evil thereof.[21]

---

[18] 32. *For after all these things do the Gentiles seek.* Jesus contrasts the Jews (to whom he is speaking) with the gentiles and their materialistic behavior.

[19] 33. *and all these things shall be added unto you.* Cf. Psalm 37:4: *And rely upon HaShem for your enjoyments, for He will grant you the desires of your heart.*

[20] 34. *Take therefore no thought for the morrow: for the morrow shall take thought for the things of itself.* Rabbi Eliezer said, "He who has only a morsel of bread in his basket, and asks: 'What shall I eat tomorrow?' is a man of little faith" (*Sotah* 48b).

[21] 34. *Sufficient unto the day is the evil thereof.* Moses said to God, "Sufficient is the evil in its time!" (*Berakoth* 9b).

VII

1. Judge not, that ye be not judged.[1] *2. For with what judgment ye judge,*[2] *ye shall be judged: and with what measure ye mete, it shall be measured to you again. 3. And why beholdest thou the mote that is in thy brother's eye, but considerest not the beam that is in thine own eye? 4. Or how wilt thou say to thy brother, Let me pull out the mote out of thine eye; and, behold, a beam is in thine own eye?*[3] *5. Thou hypocrite, first cast out the beam out of thine own eye; and then shalt thou see clearly to cast out the mote out of thy brother's eye.*[4] *6. Give not that which is holy unto the dogs, neither cast ye your pearls before swine,*[5] *lest they trample them under their feet, and turn again and rend you. 7. Ask, and it shall be given you; seek, and ye shall find; knock, and it shall be opened unto you: 8. For*

---

[1] 7:1. *Judge not, that ye be not judged.* This teaching must be viewed in the light of what the Torah teaches about justice on both communal and individual levels. One of the Seven Laws of Noah is to establish courts of justice: *Judges and officers shall you appoint in all your cities* (Deut. 16:18). Only with fair and honest courts of justice, and with judges that fear and honor God, can there be a peaceful society. It cannot be overstressed how important a concept justice is in the Torah, which also commands, "Justice, justice shall you pursue" (Deut. 16:20). On a personal level, Leviticus 19:17 commands the Jew to "rebuke your neighbor again and again," which means if you see your neighbor violate one of the mitzvot of the Torah, you are commanded to reprimand him (or her). This requires judgment. We must know the Law and *halacha* and be able to try to stir the sinner's conscience and bring him to repentance. It should be pointed out that Jesus himself spent a good deal of his time judging others as well as teaching his disciples to do likewise (Matt. 10:13–14).

[2] 2. *For with what judgment ye judge.* Our Rabbis taught, "He who judges his neighbor favorably is himself judged favorably" (*Shabbat* 127b).

[3] 4. *a beam is in thine own eye?* Rabbi Tarfon said, "for if one says to him: 'Remove the speck from between your eyes,' he would answer: 'Remove the beam from between your eyes!'" (*Arachin* 16b).

[4] 5. *the mote out of thy brother's eye.* The Oxyrhynchus Papyrus 1, Logion 1, a very early manuscript, has "And then you will see clearly to take out the speck that is in your neighbor's eye."

[5] 6. *Give not that which is holy unto the dogs, neither cast ye your pearls before swine.* Here Jesus is alluding to gentiles as dogs and swine (also cf. Matthew 15:26).

every one that asketh receiveth; and he that seeketh findeth; and to him that knocketh it shall be opened. 9. Or what man is there of you, whom if his son ask bread, will he give him a stone? 10. Or if he ask a fish, will he give him a serpent? 11. If ye then, being evil, know how to give good gifts unto your children, how much more shall your Father which is in heaven give good things to them that ask him? 12. Therefore all things whatsoever ye would that men should do to you, do ye even so to them: for this is the law and the prophets.[6] *13. Enter ye in at the strait gate: for wide is the gate,*

---

[6] *12. Therefore all things whatsoever ye would that men should do to you, do ye even so to them: for this is the law and the prophets.* This is one of the best known of all of Jesus's teachings, the Golden Rule. This is not an original teaching of Jesus, but can be found in the Torah (Leviticus 19:18), the Apocrypha (Tobit 4:15), and the Talmud. Rabbi Hillel, who was one of the great teachers of Torah in the generation before Jesus, was asked by a Noahide to teach him the Law "standing on one foot," in other words, to teach him quickly. Rabbi Hillel said to him, "What is hateful to you, do not do to your neighbor. That is the whole Torah; the rest is commentary. Go study!" (*Shabbat* 31a).

Rabbi S.R. Hirsch, in his commentary on Leviticus 19:18, said, "This is the maxim that must guide all our social behavior in thought, word and deed. The noblest fundamental attitude toward God and man is ... 'love' ... Hillel's statement indeed sums up the content of the whole Law, which, after all, is simply the teaching to shun anything that would be inimical to our own life's happiness or to that of all other creatures which enjoy existence in this world along with us. But of course the Law does not leave it to the subjective, limited views and vague emotions of man to decide what is inimical to our own welfare and to that of our fellow creatures; it has given us for this purpose a standard revealed by the wisdom and insight of God. This is what Hillel called 'its explanation'; this is the commentary on the statement which is to be derived from the Law. Thus, *Rashi* said; 'Only by studying the rest of the Torah can we find out what is truly hateful to us.' Of course, if one interprets Hillel's dictum simply as, "Do not do to others what you would not want others to do to you" and transforms this wise adage into a maxim of practical expediency: "If you do not want others to do you harm, you must also not harm them, for violence begets violence and wrong begets wrong; therefore, he who does not wish to be wronged himself must also do no wrong to others," then, of course, one has not only failed to convey the true content of our Divine Law but has not even set forth a lesson in 'ethics.' In that case one has taught only expediency and elevated calculating selfishness to be the guiding principle for all of human conduct ..." (Hirsch, *T'rumath Tzvi*, 455–56).

*and broad is the way,*⁷ *that leadeth to destruction, and many there be which go in thereat: 14. Because strait is the gate, and narrow is the way, which leadeth unto life, and few there be that find it. 15. Beware of false prophets, which come to you in sheep's clothing, but inwardly they are ravening wolves.*⁸ *16. Ye shall know them by their fruits. Do men gather grapes of thorns, or figs of thistles? 17. Even so every good tree bringeth forth good fruit; but a corrupt tree bringeth forth evil fruit. 18. A good tree cannot bring forth evil fruit, neither can a corrupt tree bring forth good fruit. 19. Every tree that bringeth not forth good fruit is hewn down, and cast into the fire. 20. Wherefore by their fruits ye shall know them.*⁹ *21. Not every one that saith unto me, lord, lord, shall enter into the kingdom of heaven; but he that doeth the will of my Father which is in heaven.*¹⁰ *22. Many will say to me in that day, Lord, Lord,*

---

⁷ *13. Enter ye in at the strait gate: for wide is the gate, and broad is the way.* Another of Jesus's most famous sayings that has been edited. Some of the oldest Greek manuscripts, as well as Clement and Origen, have *for the way is wide and easy*. (They omit ἡπύλη, "the gate.") Other manuscripts, including Sinaiticus and Vaticanus, have *Enter through the narrow gate; for the gate is wide and the road is easy.*

    א, it (some MSS.), Clement, and Origen have *for the way is wide and easy.*
    Include *Enter through the narrow gate; for the gate is wide and the road is easy*: א, B, C, W, Θ, λ, φ, it (some MSS.), vg, sy^c, sy^p, sa, bo

⁸ *15. Beware of false prophets, which come to you in sheep's clothing, but inwardly they are ravening wolves.* We cannot help but think of the Christians describing Jesus as "the lamb of God." Nittai of Abel said, "Distance yourself from a bad neighbor; do not associate with a wicked person; and do not despair of retribution" (*Pirkei Avot* 1:7).

⁹ *20. Wherefore by their fruits ye shall know them.* Cf. Rabbi Chanina ben Dosa, who said, "If the spirit of one's fellow is pleased with him, the spirit of the Omnipresent is pleased with him; but if the spirit of one's fellows is not pleased with him, the spirit of the Omnipresent is not pleased with him" (*Pirkei Avot* 3:13).

¹⁰ *21. he that doeth the will of my Father which is in heaven.* The "will" of God is the Torah, the legal and moral code he gave to mankind. It is important to note that Matthew 7:21–23 is a complete refutation of Christian theology. Calling Jesus "lord" and doing works in his name is, according to Jesus, no guarantee to eternal life. Only by keeping the Torah can one enter into *Olam ha-Bah*, the

have we not prophesied in thy name? and in thy name have cast out devils? and in thy name done many wonderful works? 23. And then will I profess unto them, I never knew you:[11] *depart from me, ye that work iniquity.*[12] *24. Therefore whosoever heareth these sayings of mine, and doeth them, I will liken him unto a wise man, which built his house upon a rock: 25. And the rain descended, and the floods came, and the winds blew, and beat upon that house; and it fell not: for it was founded upon a rock. 26. And every one that heareth these sayings of mine, and doeth them not, shall be likened unto a foolish man, which built his house upon the sand: 27. And the rain descended, and the floods came, and the winds blew, and beat upon that house; and it fell: and great was the fall of it. 28. And it came to pass, when Jesus had ended these sayings, the people were astonished at his doctrine:*[13] *29. For he taught*

World to Come (cf. Matthew 19:17, Mark 12:28–29, Luke 10:25–28).

[11] 23. *And then will I profess unto them, I never knew you.* Rabbi Elazar the Mada'ite said, "One who desecrates sacred things, who disgraces the Festivals, who humiliates his fellow in public, who nullifies the covenant of our forefather Abraham, or who perverts the Torah contrary to the *halacha*; though he may have Torah and good deeds, he has no share in the World to Come" (*Pirkei Avot* 3:15). According to the New Testament, Jesus himself did most of these things. He committed violence in the temple (John 2:14–15), violated the Sabbath (Matthew 12:1–13), humiliated his parents (Matthew 12:46–50, Luke 2:48–49, and John 2:3–4), and perverted the Torah, contrary to the *halacha* (Mark 7:18–19, Mark 10:11–12). The only thing Jesus did not do was to nullify the covenant with Abraham (circumcision).

[12] 23. *ye that work iniquity.* The Greek here at the end of verse 23—ἐργαζόμενοι τὴν ἀνομίαν—translates as "you that work against the Jewish Law." It is not always translated this way. In the KJV, it is "iniquity," and in the NIV it is "you evildoers." The Greek word here, ἀνομίαν, is the same word found in Matthew 5:17, νόμον, which is the word for Law (Torah) with the negative prefix "α" (as in English with "moral" and "amoral"). In these three verses (7:21–23), Jesus refutes the later Christian teaching that one must "accept Jesus as Lord" in order to have salvation, for Jesus himself teaches that, in order to have salvation, one must keep the Law. Rabbi Hillel said, "One who has gained himself Torah knowledge, has gained himself the life of the World to Come" (*Pirkei Avot* 2:8).

[13] 28. *And it came to pass, when Jesus had ended these sayings, the people were astonished at his doctrine.* The Sermon in the Mount closes with the parable of the wise man building his house on the rock. To put this parable in perspective,

them as one having authority, and not as the scribes.

---

we turn to the first Psalm: *The praises of Man are that he walked not in the counsel of the wicked, and stood not in the path of the sinful, and sat not in the session of scorners. But his desire is in the Torah of HaShem, and in his Torah he meditates day and night. He shall be like a tree replanted by streams of water that yields its fruit in due season, and whose leaf never withers. And everything he does will succeed. Not so the wicked: they are like the chaff which the wind drives away. Therefore the wicked shall not be vindicated in judgment, nor the sinful in the assembly of the righteous. For HaShem recognizes the way of the righteous, while the way of the wicked is doomed.* This teaching, which follows the one before it about Jesus turning away those who do not keep the Torah, shows that only those who base their faith on the Torah (rather than Gnostic theology) will be considered righteous.

VIII

1. When he was come down from the mountain, great multitudes followed him. 2. And, behold, there came a leper and worshiped him,[1] *saying, Lord, if thou wilt, thou canst make me clean. 3. And Jesus put forth his hand, and touched him, saying, I will; be thou clean. And immediately his leprosy was cleansed.*[2] *4. And Jesus saith unto him, See thou tell no man;*[3] *but go thy way, shew*

---

[1] 8:2. *there came a leper and worshiped him.* With chapter eight, the mood and tone of Matthew suddenly and suspiciously change. After reading his long discourse on the Torah in the Sermon on the Mount, we now come to the miracle stories that were so popular with the Gnostic Christians as well as a sudden attitude reversal by Jesus concerning Jews and gentiles. In the previous three chapters (the Sermon on the Mount), Jesus focused the Torah and Jewish ethics and told his Jewish audience not to follow the immoral customs of the gentiles (cf. 5:47, 6:7, 32), using non-Jews as examples of sinful behavior. Now, in chapter eight, he suddenly starts praising the gentiles and condemning the "sons of the kingdom" (the Jews; 8:10–12) while he is running around doing "miracles." The miracle stories have more in common with the stories in the lesser-known Gnostic gospels, such as the Infancy Gospel of Thomas (a work quoted by Irenaeus, which means it is at least as old as the canonical gospels) or the Infancy Gospel (or *Protevangelion*) of James, two works of the mid-second century that were quoted by early church fathers.

Here is an example from the Infancy Gospel of Thomas, 16:1–4, where the young Jesus follows his father around and covers for Joseph's incompetence. "And Joseph, wheresoever he went in the city, took the lord Jesus with him, where he was sent for to work to make gates, or milk-pails, or sieves, or boxes; the lord Jesus was with him wheresoever he went. And as often as Joseph had anything in his work, to make longer or shorter, or wider, or narrower, the lord Jesus would stretch his hand towards it. And presently it became as Joseph would have it. So that he had no need to finish anything with his own hands, for he was not very skillful at his carpenter's trade." (*Lost Books of the Bible.* New York: Bell Publishing Co., 1979, 53.) These were the sorts of miracle stories that so delighted the second-century Gnostics and would be passed down through the centuries. Even today, there are oral traditions about Jesus that have no written tradition, one example being the story of the dogwood tree being used to make the cross, Jesus miraculously stunting its growth forevermore, and dogwood blossom being a remembrance of the Crucifixion.

[2] 3. *And immediately his leprosy was cleansed.* This miracle had been done before. See the *Tanach* (2 Kings 5:1–14).

[3] 4. *See thou tell no man.* Seeing how "great multitudes" are following his ev-

thyself to the priest, and offer the gift that Moses commanded,[4] *for a testimony unto them. 5. And when Jesus was entered into Capernaum, there came unto him a centurion, beseeching him, 6. And saying, Lord, my servant lieth at home sick of the palsy, grievously tormented. 7. And Jesus saith unto him, I will come and heal him. 8. The centurion answered and said, Lord, I am not worthy that thou shouldest come under my roof: but speak the word only, and my servant shall be healed. 9. For I am a man under authority, having soldiers under me: and I say to this man, Go, and he goeth; and to another, Come, and he cometh; and to my servant, Do this, and he doeth it. 10. When Jesus heard it, he marveled, and said to them that followed, Verily I say unto you, I have not found so great faith, no, not in Israel.*[5] *11. And I say unto you, That many shall come from the east and west, and shall sit down with Abraham, and Isaac, and Jacob, in the kingdom of heaven. 12. But the children of the kingdom shall be cast out into outer darkness:*[6] *there shall be weeping and gnashing of teeth. 13.*

---

ery move (cf. 8:1, 9:8), it makes little sense for Jesus to ask the man not to tell anyone.

[4] 4. *shew thyself to the priest, and offer the gift that Moses commanded.* Jesus performs a miracle and also goes to the temple to offer a sacrifice as the Torah commands. He asks the man not to tell anyone, which instruction the man promptly disobeys. The Christian explanation for this behavior is that Jesus had not "fulfilled" the Law at this time. In Mark 7:18–19, however, Christians say that Jesus declared all foods clean, nullifying the kosher laws; this says that since Jesus was God, he can change the Law at his whim.

[5] 10. *not found so great faith, no, not in Israel.* Many of the oldest manuscripts have "in no one in Israel," and others have "not even in Israel." Verses with multiple corruptions should raise a red flag. More than likely, this was an oral tradition that developed with the later Hellenistic movement, which would explain the sudden anti-Jewish sentiment in the text.

[6] 12. *But the children of the kingdom shall be cast out into outer darkness.* After the Sermon on the Mount, where Jesus was contrasting the behavior of the gentiles with the Jews (*Ye are the salt of the earth ... Ye are the light of the world*, Matthew 5:13–14; "But when ye pray, use not vain repetitions, as the Gentiles do," Matthew 6:7), suddenly the tone changes with the miracle stories. The implication now is that the gentiles will be blessed and have salvation, whereas the Jews, the "children of the kingdom," the "salt of the earth," and "the light of the world" will be cast into hell. This is one of the "*Q*" verses (cf. Luke 13:28–29)

And Jesus said unto the centurion, Go thy way; and as thou hast believed, so be it done unto thee. And his servant was healed in the selfsame hour.[7] *14. And when Jesus was come into Peter's house, he saw his wife's mother laid, and sick of a fever. 15. And he touched her hand, and the fever left her: and she arose, and ministered unto them. 16. When the even was come, they brought unto him many that were possessed with devils: and he cast out the spirits with his word, and healed all that were sick: 17. That it might be fulfilled which was spoken by Esaias the prophet, saying, Himself took our infirmities, and bare our sicknesses.*[8] *18. Now when Jesus saw great multitudes about him, he gave commandment to depart unto the other side. 19. And a certain scribe came, and said unto him, Master, I will follow thee whithersoever thou goest. 20. And Jesus saith unto him, The foxes have holes, and the birds of the air have nests; but the Son of man hath not where to lay his head. 21. And another of his disciples said unto him, Lord, suffer me first to*

---

that were added to the narrative of Matthew at fortuitous locations, as where gentiles are praised.

[7] 13. *And his servant was healed in the selfsame hour.* Another corrupted text. Some of the older manuscripts have "and when the centurion returned to his house in that hour he found the servant well" (cf. Luke 7:10); other manuscripts (Sinaiticus, Vaticanus, old Italic, etc.) have "and the servant was healed in that hour." When a story such as the centurion story (Matt. 8:5–18) has altered verses to the extent of verses 10 and 13, plus the narrative is different from a similar story in Luke 7:1–10, makes this story highly suspect.

א, C, Θ, and λ, all have *and when the centurion returned to his house in that hour he found the servant well*, cf. Luke 7:10
And the servant was healed in that hour: א, B, W, φ, it, vg, sy^c, sy^s, sy^p, sa, bo

[8] 17. *Himself took our infirmities, and bare our sicknesses.* This passage from Isaiah 53 speaks about Israel (cf. *Rashi* on Isaiah 52:13): "Behold, My servant will succeed; he will be exalted and become high and exceedingly lofty. Just as multitudes were astonished over you, [saying,] 'His appearance is too marred to be a man's, and his visage to be human,' so will the many nations exclaim about him, and kings will shut their mouths [in amazement], for they will see that which had never been told to them, and will perceive things they had never heard." Throughout Isaiah, as in Isaiah 41:8, 44:1, and 44:21, Israel is described as HaShem's servant. The verb in Matthew for "bare," ἐβάσταστν, also means "removed" or "took away," which fits the passage. Isaiah 53:4 has the servant *bearing* the people's sins, not curing them.

*go and bury my father.*⁹ *22. But Jesus said unto him, Follow me; and let the dead bury their dead.*¹⁰ *23. And when he was entered into a ship, his disciples followed him. 24. And, behold, there arose a great tempest in the sea, insomuch that the ship was covered with the waves: but he was asleep. 25. And his disciples came to him, and awoke him, saying, Lord, save us: we perish. 26. And he saith unto them, Why are ye fearful, O ye of little faith? Then he arose, and rebuked the winds and the sea; and there was a great calm. 27. But the men marvelled, saying, What manner of man is this, that even the winds and the sea obey him! 28. And when he was come to the other side into the country of the Gergesenes,*¹¹ *there met him two possessed with devils, coming out of the tombs, exceeding fierce, so that no man might pass by that way. 29. And, behold, they cried out, saying, What have we to do with thee, Jesus, thou Son of God? art thou come hither to torment us before the time? 30. And there was a good way off from them an herd of many swine feeding. 31. So the devils besought him, saying, If thou cast us out, suffer us to go away into the herd of swine. 32. And he said unto them, Go. And when they were come out, they went into the herd of swine: and, behold, the whole herd of swine ran violently down a steep place into the sea, and perished in the waters. 33. And they that kept them fled, and went their ways into the city, and told every thing, and what was befallen to the possessed of the devils. 34. And, behold, the whole city came out to meet Jesus: and when they saw*

---

⁹ 21. *go and bury my father.* Seeing how this was the father of one of Jesus's disciples, it seems odd that Jesus left him there unburied instead of raising him from the dead (cf. Matthew 9:18–25).

¹⁰ 22. *let the dead bury their dead.* This is a violation of two commandments: to honor your parents (Deuteronomy 5:16) and to bury the dead (Deuteronomy 21:23). The Torah teaches that we should have utmost respect for the dead (*kevod hamet*). We must never leave the body of a recently deceased person alone for any reason, most certainly not our parent.

¹¹ 28. *Gergesenes.* Sinaiticus, Vaticanus, and other early texts have the word *Gadarenes*. Other texts have *Gerasenes*.
    Gadarenes: ℵ, B, C, Θ, sy^s, sy^p
    Gergesenes: 𝕂, W, λ, φ, bo
    Gerasenes: it, vg, sa

him, they besought him that he would depart out of their coasts.[12]

---

[12] 34. *they besought him that he would depart out of their coasts.* This was the Miracle of the Purloined Pork. After Jesus destroys a herd of swine, the owners of the pigs run and tell everyone in the local town what Jesus did. The town's inhabitants then beg Jesus to leave before he destroys any more property. Perhaps Jesus did not like the idea of herds of swine in *Eretz Yisrael*, or that the local Jews should not be keeping herds of swine in the first place. Some commentators point out that these were probably pigs raised to feed the Roman garrisons, but even so, why would Jesus destroy property that did not belong to him?

IX

1. And he entered into a ship, and passed over, and came into his own city. 2. And, behold, they brought to him a man sick of the palsy, lying on a bed: and Jesus seeing their faith said unto the sick of the palsy; Son, be of good cheer; thy sins be forgiven thee. 3. And, behold, certain of the scribes said within themselves, This man blasphemeth. 4. And Jesus knowing their thoughts[1] said, Wherefore think ye evil in your hearts? 5. For whether is easier, to say,[2] Thy sins be forgiven thee;[3] or to say, Arise, and walk? 6. But that ye may know that the Son of man hath power on earth to forgive sins, (then saith he to the sick of the palsy,) Arise, take up thy bed, and go unto thine house. 7. And he arose, and departed to his house. 8. But when the multitudes saw it, they marvelled, and glorified God, which had given such power unto men. 9. And as Jesus passed forth from thence, he saw a man, named Matthew, sitting at the receipt of custom: and he saith unto him, Follow me. And he arose, and followed him. 10. And it came to pass, as Jesus sat at meat in the house, behold, many publicans and sinners came and sat down with him and his disciples.[4] 11. And when the Pharisees saw it, they said unto his disciples, Why eateth your

---

[1] *9:4. And Jesus knowing their thoughts.* Vaticanus and a few other texts (B, Θ, λ, sy^p, and sa) have "perceiving" rather than "knowing" (seeing).

[2] *5. For whether is easier, to say.* The Greek text is essentially the same in Matthew 9:5–7, Mark 2:9–12, and Luke 5:23–25. Given the three different styles of writing in these three gospels, this can only be explained that the synoptic gospels either drew on the same material or were corrupted by the Diatesseron.

[3] *5. Thy sins be forgiven thee.* Sinaiticus, Vaticanus, and Beaze, along with other early texts, have *your sins are forgiven.*

[4] 10. *many publicans and sinners came and sat down with him and his disciples.* Cf. Psalm 1:1–2: *The praises of Man are that he walked not in the counsel of the wicked, (a)nd stood not in the path of the sinful, and sat not in the session of scorners. But his desire is in the Torah of HaShem, and in his Torah he meditates day and night.* One of the criticisms of the Pharisees towards Jesus was that Jesus seemed to spend more time with the wicked and sinful than he did with the pious. One of the hallmarks of a righteous person is that they do not associate with the wicked.

Master with publicans and sinners?[5] 12. But when Jesus heard that, he said unto them, They that be whole need not a physician, but they that are sick. 13. But go ye and learn what that meaneth, I will have mercy, and not sacrifice:[6] for I am not come to call the righteous, but sinners to repentance. 14. Then came to him the disciples of John, saying, Why do we and the Pharisees fast oft,[7] but thy disciples fast not? 15. And Jesus said unto them, Can the children of the bridechamber mourn, as long as the bridegroom is with them? but the days will come, when the bridegroom shall be taken from them, and then shall they fast. 16. No man putteth a piece of new cloth unto an old garment, for that which is put in to fill it up taketh from the garment, and the rent is made worse. 17. Neither do men put new wine into old bottles: else the bottles break, and the wine runneth out, and the bottles perish: but they put new wine into new bottles, and both are preserved.[8] 18. While he spake these things unto them, behold, there came a certain ruler, and worshipped him,[9] saying, My daughter is even now dead: but come and lay thy hand upon her, and she shall live. 19. And Jesus arose, and followed him, and so did his disciples. 20. And, behold, a woman, which was diseased with an issue of blood twelve years, came behind him, and touched the hem of his garment: 21. For she said within herself, If I may but touch his garment, I shall be

---

[5] 11. *Why eateth your Master with publicans and sinners?* Cf. note 4, above. Rabbi Dosa ben Harkinas said, "Late morning sleep, midday wine, children's chatter, and sitting in the assemblies of the ignorant, remove a man from the world" (*Pirkei Avot* 3:14).

[6] 13. *I will have mercy, and not sacrifice.* The entire verse from Hosea 6:6 reads, *For I desire kindness, not sacrifice; and knowledge of God more than burnt-offerings.* The context is important here, for it adds the knowledge of God (Torah) as well as kindness.

[7] 14. *Why do we and the Pharisees fast oft (often).* Both Sinaiticus and Vaticanus omit the word "often."

[8] 17. *but they put new wine into new bottles, and both are preserved.* This teaching has been a continuing problem for theologians, for it implies that Judaism, the "old" wine, would be preserved along with the "new" wine, or Christianity.

[9] 18. *and worshiped him.* Cf. commentary on Matthew 2:2 for the word "worship."

whole. 22. But Jesus turned him about, and when he saw her,[10] he said, Daughter, be of good comfort; thy faith hath made thee whole. And the woman was made whole from that hour. 23. And when Jesus came into the ruler's house, and saw the minstrels and the people making a noise, 24. He said unto them, Give place: for the maid is not dead, but sleepeth. And they laughed him to scorn. 25. But when the people were put forth, he went in, and took her by the hand, and the maid arose. 26. And the fame hereof went abroad into all that land. 27. And when Jesus departed thence, two blind men followed him, crying, and saying, Thou Son of David, have mercy on us. 28. And when he was come into the house, the blind men came to him: and Jesus saith unto them, Believe ye that I am able to do this? They said unto him, Yea, Lord. 29. Then touched he their eyes, saying, According to your faith be it unto you. 30. And their eyes were opened; and Jesus straitly charged them, saying, See that no man know it.[11] 31. But they, when they were departed, spread abroad his fame in all that country. 32. As they went out, behold, they brought to him a dumb man possessed with a devil. 33. And when the devil was cast out, the dumb spake: and the multitudes marvelled, saying, It was never so seen in Israel. 34. But the Pharisees said, He casteth out devils through the prince of the devils.[12] 35. And Jesus went about all the cities and villages, teaching In their synagogues, and preaching the gospel of the

---

[10] 22. *But Jesus turned him about, and when he saw her.* Cf. Mark 5:30, where Jesus did not know who touched his clothes. This was left out of Matthew's account, no doubt because it made Jesus appear ignorant.

[11] 30. *and Jesus straitly charged them, saying, See that no man know it.* The writer of Matthew disobeyed Jesus's teaching here, making sure that *everyone* knew it.

[12] 34. *But the Pharisees said, He casteth out devils through the prince of the devils.* Sinaiticus and Vaticanus, along with many other early texts, have *But the Pharisees said, "By the ruler of the demons he casts out the demons.* Codex Bezae, the Diatessaron, and several Old Latin manuscripts omit this verse entirely. That many of the early manuscripts omit this verse makes it highly suspect that it is original.

> *But the Pharisees said, By the ruler of the demons he casts out the demons":* 𝕂, ℵ, B, C, λ, φ, it (some MSS.), vg, sy^p, sa, bo
> Omit verse 34: D, it (some MSS.), sy^s, Diatessaron.

kingdom, and healing every sickness and every disease among the people. 36. But when he saw the multitudes, he was moved with compassion on them, because they fainted, and were scattered abroad, as sheep having no shepherd. 37. Then saith he unto his disciples, The harvest truly is plenteous, but the labourers are few; 38. Pray ye therefore the Lord of the harvest, that he will send forth labourers into his harvest.

X

1. And when he had called unto him his twelve disciples, he gave them power against unclean spirits, to cast them out, and to heal all manner of sickness and all manner of disease.[1] 2. Now the names of the twelve apostles are these; The first, Simon, who is called Peter, and Andrew his brother; James the son of Zebedee, and John his brother; 3. Philip, and Bartholomew; Thomas, and Matthew the publican; James the son of Alphaeus, and Lebbaeus, whose surname was Thaddaeus;[2] 4. Simon the Canaanite, and Judas Iscariot, who also betrayed him. 5. These twelve Jesus sent forth, and commanded them, saying, Go not into the way of the Gentiles,[3] and into any city of the Samaritans enter ye not: 6. But

---

[1] *10:1. he gave them power against unclean spirits, to cast them out, and to heal all manner of sickness and all manner of disease.* Here, Jesus teaches his disciples how to do "miracles." Every miracle Jesus supposedly performed had been performed by the earlier prophets, if not the exact miracle, at least something quite similar. For instance, Elisha heals a man of leprosy in 2 Kings 5:1–14, he feeds a multitude with a few loaves and still has some left over in 2 Kings 4:42–44, he makes an axe head float in 2 Kings 6:6, and both Elijah and Elisha raise people from the dead in 1 Kings 17:17–24, 2 Kings 4:8–37, and 2 Kings 13:21.

Herein lies the problem with Christian "faith in Jesus." Since these same miracles had been performed by earlier prophets, it is hard to understand why Christians demand that Jesus was "God incarnate" because he performed miracles. This is the root of Christian idolatry: Christians do not "believe in God." Rather, they "believe Jesus was God;" that is, their faith is rooted in the Gnostic belief that Jesus was a divine being sent down from heaven.

[2] *3. and Lebbaeus, whose surname was Thaddaeus.* Sinaiticus and Vaticanus and other early manuscripts have *and Thaddaeus*, Bezae has *Lebbaeus*, other manuscripts have *Lebbaeus called Thaddaeus*, some Old Latin manuscripts have *Judas Zelotes*, and a few have added *Judas the son of James* after "Cananaean" in verse 4.

    and Thaddaeus: ℵ, B, φ, it (some MSS.), vg, sa, bo
    Lebbaeus: D
    Lebbaeus called Thaddaeus: 𝕂, C?, W, Θ, λ, sy^p
    Judas Zelotes: it (some MSS.)
    Add *Judas the son of James* after "Cananaean" in verse 4: sy^s

[3] *5. Go not into the way of the Gentiles.* Jesus tells his disciples not to reach out

go rather to the lost sheep of the house of Israel. 7. And as ye go, preach, saying, The kingdom of heaven is at hand. 8. Heal the sick, cleanse the lepers, raise the dead, cast out devils: freely ye have received, freely give. 9. Provide neither gold, nor silver, nor brass in your purses, 10. Nor scrip for your journey, neither two coats, neither shoes, nor yet staves: for the workman is worthy of his meat. 11. And into whatsoever city or town ye shall enter, enquire who in it is worthy; and there abide till ye go thence. 12. And when ye come into an house, salute it. 13. And if the house be worthy, let your peace come upon it: but if it be not worthy, let your peace return to you. 14. And whosoever shall not receive you, nor hear your words, when ye depart out of that house or city, shake off the dust of your feet. 15. Verily I say unto you, It shall be more tolerable for the land of Sodom and Gomorrha in the day of judgment, than for that city. 16. Behold, I send you forth as sheep in the midst of wolves: be ye therefore wise as serpents, and harmless as doves. 17. But beware of men: for they will deliver you up to the councils, and they will scourge you in their synagogues; 18. And ye shall be brought before governors and kings for my sake,[4] for a testimony against them and the Gentiles. 19. But when they deliver you up, take no thought how or what ye shall speak: for it shall be given you in that same hour what ye shall speak. 20. For it is not ye that speak, but the Spirit of your Father which speaketh in you. 21. And the brother shall deliver up the brother to death, and the father the child: and the children shall rise up against their parents, and cause them to be put to death. 22. And ye shall be hated of all men for my name's sake:[5] but he that endureth to the end shall be saved. 23. But when they persecute you in this city, flee ye into another: for verily I say unto you, Ye shall not have gone over the cities of

---

to the gentiles. This is the second of the long monologues in Matthew, and once again the focus and tone about the gentiles shifts.

[4] 18. *And ye shall be brought before governors and kings for my sake.* In the past many Jews were brought before Christian rulers to force them to denounce their faith.

[5] 22. *And ye shall be hated of all men for my name's sake.* Jews have been hated and persecuted in the name of Jesus for nearly two thousand years.

*Israel, till the Son of man be come.*⁶ 24. *The disciple is not above his master, nor the servant above his lord. 25. It is enough for the disciple that he be as his master, and the servant as his lord. If they have called the master of the house Beelzebub, how much more shall they call them of his household? 26. Fear them not therefore: for there is nothing covered, that shall not be revealed and hid, that shall not be known.*⁷ 27. *What I tell you in darkness, that speak ye in light:*⁸ *and what ye hear in the ear, that preach ye upon the housetops. 28. And fear not them which kill the body, but are not able to kill the soul: but rather fear him which is able to destroy both soul and body in hell. 29. Are not two sparrows sold for a farthing? and one of them shall not fall on the ground without your Father. 30. But the very hairs of your head are all numbered. 31. Fear ye not therefore, ye are of more value than many sparrows. 32. Whosoever therefore shall confess me before men, him will I confess also before my Father which is in heaven. 33. But whosoever shall deny me before men, him will I also deny before my Father which is in heaven.*⁹ 34. *Think not that I am come*

---

⁶ 23. *for verily I say unto you, Ye shall not have gone over the cities of Israel, till the Son of man be come.* Another "prophecy" of Jesus that did not come true.

⁷ 26. *Fear them not therefore: for there is nothing covered, that shall not be revealed; and hid, that shall not be known.* Oxyrhynchus Papyrus 654, Logion 4. reads, "Jesus said, 'Everything that is not before you, and what is hidden from you will be revealed to you. For there is nothing hidden that will not be revealed, nor buried, that will not be raised.'"

⁸ 27. *What I tell you in darkness, that speak ye in light ... fear not them which kill the body, but are not able to kill the soul.* Here Jesus uses Gnostic symbolism; the dualism of light/darkness, soul/body. Rudolf Bultmann writes, "Aside from the terms for mythological figures, the terminology in which dualism is expressed shows extensive Gnostic influence. This is most apparent in John, whose language is governed by the antithesis 'light–darkness.' But the rest of the New Testament also knows this contrast (Rom. 13:12; I Thess. 5:4f; II Cor. [6:14]; Col. 1:12f.; Eph. 5:8ff.; 6:12; I Pet. 2:9; cf. I Clem. 36:2; II Clem. 1:4, Barn. 14:5f.; 18:1; Ign. Rom. 6:2; Phld. 2:1)", (*Theology of the New Testament*, New York: Charles Scribner's Sons, 1951, §15, 173.)

⁹ 33. *I also deny before my Father which is in heaven.* There is nothing in the Torah that this can apply to. What does it mean to "deny" Jesus? To believe that Jesus was God was a violation of Torah, and this contradicts Jesus's own teaching as given in Matthew 7:21–23.

to send peace on earth:[10] I came not to Send peace, but a sword. 35. For I am come to set a man at variance[11] against his father, and the daughter against her mother, and the daughter in law against her mother in law.[12] 36. And a man's foes shall be they of his own household. 37. He that loveth father or mother more than me is not worthy of me:[13] and he that loveth son or daughter more than me is not worthy of me. 38. And he that taketh not his cross, and followeth after me, is not worthy of me. 39. He that findeth his life shall lose it: and he that loseth his life for my sake shall find it. 40. He that receiveth you receiveth me, and he that receiveth me receiveth him that sent me. 41. He that receiveth a prophet in the name of a prophet shall receive a prophet's reward; and he that receiveth a righteous man in the name of a righteous man shall receive a righteous man's reward. 42. And whosoever shall give to drink unto one of these little ones a cup of cold water only in the name of a disciple, verily I say unto you, he shall in no wise lose his reward.

---

[10] 34. *Think not that I am come to send peace on earth.* One of the things that the real Messiah will do will be to bring peace on earth (Isaiah 2:2–4).

[11] 35. *For I am come to set a man at variance.* This verse, from Micah 7:6, deals with the false prophets in whom the people have put their trust: *On the day of your expectation, your punishment will come* (Micah 7:4). Christians believe that they will be "saved" by basing their faith that Jesus was God, or at the very least, "His son." *As for me, I put my hope in HaShem and await the God of my salvation* (Micah 7:7). Only by putting one's faith in HaShem and His Torah can one have salvation.

[12] 35. *and the daughter in law against her mother in law.* "It has been taught: R. Nehorai said: In the generation when Messiah comes, young men will insult the old, and old men will stand before the young [to give them honor]; daughters will rise up against their mothers, and daughters-in-law against their mothers-in-law. The people shall be dog-faced, and a son will not be abashed in his father's presence" (*Sanhedrin* 97a). Jesus admits that he will be the cause of the world's problems, not the real messiah who comes to fix them. "It has been taught, R. Nehemiah [150 CE] said: In the generation of the Messiah's coming impudence will increase, esteem be perverted … and the Kingdom will be converted to heresy" (*Sanhedrin* 97b). The "kingdom," means the Roman empire, which converted to Christianity. Jesus's teachings will be the cause of heresy.

[13] 37. *He that loveth father or mother more than me is not worthy of me.* Here Jesus teaches disrespect of one's parents, a violation of the Torah.

XI

1. And it came to pass, when Jesus had made an end of commanding his twelve disciples, he departed thence to teach and to preach in their cities. 2. Now when John had heard in the prison the works of Christ, he sent two of his disciples, 3. And said unto him, Art thou he that should come, or do we look for another?[1] 4. Jesus answered and said unto them, Go and shew John again those things which ye do hear and see: 5. The blind receive their sight, and the lame walk, the lepers are cleansed, and the deaf hear, the dead are raised up, and the poor have the gospel preached to them. 6. And

---

[1] 11:3. *Art thou he that should come, or do we look for another?* Many of the Jews who first supported Jesus are now having doubts. One such is John the Baptist, who sends two of his disciples to ask a straightforward question: "Are you the Messiah or not?" They are asking Jesus to show a sign as demanded by God (Deuteronomy 18:15–22). Jesus gives them a vague answer about all the miracles he did, but he really does not answer the question.

According to *Rambam* (*Hilchot Melachim* 11:4), he says, "If a king will arise from the House of David who diligently contemplates the Torah and observes its mitzvot as prescribed by the Written Law and the Oral Law as David, his ancestor, compels all of Israel to walk in [the way of the Torah] and rectify the breaches [in its observance], and fights the wars of God, we may, with assurance, consider him HaMashiach. If he succeeds in the above, builds the Temple in its place, and gathers the dispersed of Israel, he is definitely the Messiah. He will then improve the entire world, [motivating] all the nations to serve God together as [Zephaniah 3:9] states: 'I will make the people pure of speech that they all will call upon the Name of God and serve Him with one purpose.' If he did not succeed to this degree or he was killed, he surely is not [the redeemer] promised by the Torah. [Rather,] he should be considered as all the other proper and complete kings of the Davidic dynasty who died. God only caused him to arise in order to test many, as [Daniel 11:35] states; 'and some of the wise men will stumble, to try them, to refine, and to clarify until the appointed time, because the set time is in the future.' Can there be a greater stumbling block than [Christianity]? All the prophets spoke of Mashiach as the redeemer of Israel and their savior who would gather their dispersed and strengthen their [observance of] the mitzvot. [In contrast, Christianity] caused the Jews to be slain by the sword, their remnants to be scattered and humbled, the Torah to be altered, and the majority of the world to err and serve a god other than the Lord ... When the true Messianic King will arise and prove successful, his [position becoming] exalted and uplifted, they will all return and realize that their ancestors endowed them with a false heritage and their prophets and ancestors caused them to err."

blessed is he, whosoever shall not be offended in me. 7. And as they departed, Jesus began to say unto the multitudes concerning John, What went ye out into the wilderness to see? A reed shaken with the wind? 8. But what went ye out for to see? A man clothed in soft raiment? behold, they that wear soft clothing are in kings' houses. 9. But what went ye out for to see? A prophet?[2] yea, I say unto you, and more than a prophet. 10. For this is he, of whom it is written, Behold, I send my messenger Before thy face,[3] which shall prepare thy way before thee. 11. Verily I say unto you, Among them that are born of women there hath not risen a greater than John the Baptist: notwithstanding, he that is least in the kingdom of heaven is greater than he. 12. And from the days of John the Baptist until now the kingdom of heaven suffereth violence, and the violent take it by force. 13. For all the prophets and the law prophesied until John. 14. And if ye will receive it, this is Elias, which was for to come.[4] 15. He that hath ears to hear, let him hear.[5] 16. But whereunto shall I liken this generation? It is like unto children sitting in the markets,

---

[2] *9. But what went ye out for to see? A prophet?* Many early texts have *What then did you go out to see? A prophet?* Other texts have *Why then did you go out? To see a prophet?*

What then did you go out to see? A prophet?: 𝕂, C, D, Θ, λ, φ, it, vg, sy^c, sy^s, sy^p, sa

Why then did you go out? To see a prophet?: א, W, bo

[3] *10. Behold, I send my messenger before thy face.* The quotation in the *Tanach* reads, *Behold, I am sending My messenger, and he will clear a path before Me* (Malachi 3:1). God's messenger of the covenant, Elijah, will come and rid the land of the wicked (Rashi). The phrases "my face" and "prepare thy way before thee" are not in the Hebrew text. Again, we are faced with the problem of either Jesus adding to the text of the *Tanach*, or later Christian scribes corrupting the text by putting words into Jesus's mouth.

[4] *14. And if ye will receive it, this is Elias, which was for to come.* Cf. John 1:21, where John says he is not Elijah, which means one of the gospel writers is not telling the truth.

[5] *15. He that hath ears to hear, let him hear.* Several early texts have *Let anyone with ears listen!* Other early manuscripts have *Let anyone with ears to hear listen!*

Let anyone with ears listen!: B, D, sy^s

Let anyone with ears to hear listen!: 𝕂, א, C, W, Θ, λ, φ, it, vg, sy^c, sy^p, sa, bo

and calling unto their fellows, 17. And saying, We have piped unto you, and ye have not danced; we have mourned unto you, and ye have not lamented. 18. For John came neither eating nor drinking, and they say, He hath a devil. 19. The Son of man came eating and drinking, and they say, Behold a man gluttonous, and a winebibber, a friend of publicans and sinners.[6] But wisdom is justified of her children.[7] 20. Then began he to upbraid the cities wherein most of his mighty works were done, because they repented not: 21. Woe unto thee, Chorazin! woe unto thee, Bethsaida! for if the mighty works, which were done in you, had been done in Tyre and Sidon, they would have repented long ago in sackcloth and ashes. 22. But I say unto you, It shall be more tolerable for Tyre and Sidon at the day of judgment, than for you. 23. And thou, Capernaum, which art exalted unto heaven, shalt be brought down to hell: for if the mighty works, which have been done in thee, had been done in Sodom, it would have remained until this day. 24. But I say unto you, That it shall be more tolerable for the land of Sodom in the day of judgment, than for thee. 25. At that time Jesus answered and said, I thank thee, O Father, Lord of heaven and earth,[8] because thou hast hid these things[9] from the wise and prudent, and hast revealed

---

[6] 19. *Behold a man gluttonous, and a wine-bibber, a friend of publicans and sinners.* Jesus enjoyed good food and good wine and by his own admission hung out with the wrong crowd. It is no wonder that with a reputation like this, it was difficult for Jesus to set the minds of many Jewish followers in agreement with all of his judgments on issues of Torah observance. As Proverbs 3:20 states, *A companion of fools will suffer harm.* Jesus hung out with fools and criticized Torah scholars.

[7] 19. *But wisdom is justified of her children.* This verse can only be understood in the context of Gnosticism. The word "wisdom" here is σοφία, or Sophia. Sophia is identified with the Gnostic theological concept of the Holy Spirit. She was the lowest of the æons, and the "mother" of the demiurge (Satan).

[8] 25. *I thank thee, O Father, Lord of heaven and earth.* In this passage, the word "thank" is the Greek word ἐξομολογοῦμαι, or "confess" (cf. Romans 14:11; Philippians 2:11). The only other time this word is translated as "thank" is in a similar prayer in Luke 10:21. This verse is the traditional Hebrew prayer, *Baruch ahtaw Adoni, Eloheinu melech haolam* (Blessed are You, HaShem, our God, King of the universe").

[9] 25. *because thou hast hid these things.* The concept of the hidden *mysteries* is another concept from Gnosticism. The present author writes, "The 'sonship' of

them unto babes. 26. Even so, Father: for so it seemed good in thy sight. 27. All things are delivered unto me of my Father: and no man knoweth the Son, but the Father; neither knoweth any man the Father, save the Son, and he to whomsoever the Son will reveal him.[10] *28. Come unto me, all ye that labour and are heavy laden, and I will give you rest. 29. Take my yoke upon you,*[11] *and learn of me; for I am meek and lowly in heart:*[12] *and ye shall find rest unto your souls. 30. For my yoke is easy, and my burden is light.*

Jesus — in fact, the very concept of the trinity itself — is a Gnostic concept of the "created" god, or *æon*. It was thought to be first expounded by the Valentinians, another popular Gnostic Christian sect during the early formative centuries of Christianity. The Valentinians developed two new *æons*: the 'Christos' and the 'Holy Spirit.' The *trinity* is one of the 'mystery' teachings of Gnostic Christianity. Neither the word *trinity* nor any language that describes God as being 'three-in-one' is found in the New Testament. According to the Gnostic Church, the secret teaching of the trinity was passed down orally from the apostles to the 'elect,' and it is one of the foundational mystery teachings of Christianity — that a Christian must have this *gnosis* of the trinity to fully 'know' God and achieve 'salvation'"(Cecil, *The Noahide Code*, 28).

[10] 27. *neither knoweth any man the Father, save the Son, and he to whomsoever the Son will reveal him.* Another Gnostic teaching of Jesus bringing the "mystery" knowledge down from heaven. According to Matthew, only Jesus has this secret knowledge of God.

[11] 29. *Take my yoke upon you.* "Rabbi Nechunia ben Hakanah says: 'If someone takes upon himself the yoke of Torah — the yoke of government and the yoke of worldly responsibilities are removed from him. But if someone throws off the yoke of Torah from himself — the yoke of government and the yoke of worldly responsibilities are placed upon him'" (*Pirkei Avos* 3:6).

[12] 29. *meek and lowly in heart.* Jesus comes across in Matthew as anything but meek and lowly of heart; if there is one word that can best describe his character, it would be *arrogant*. Cf. chapter 21, when he rides into Jerusalem and forcibly takes over the temple, or chapter 23 where he denounces the Pharisees.

XII

1. At that time Jesus went on the sabbath day through the corn;[1]

---

[1] 12:1. *At that time Jesus went on the sabbath day through the corn.* This is the one occurrence in the gospel of Matthew when Jesus actually answers a question of *halacha*. Jesus and his disciples are traveling through the grain fields on the Sabbath. The disciples are hungry, so they pick some of the grain and eat it, an act that is one of the thirty-nine *melachot*, or prohibitions of work, that a Jew cannot do on the Sabbath. When the Pharisees point this out to Jesus, he defends their actions by telling them the story from 1 Samuel 21:2–7, where David ate the showbread that was only to be eaten by the Kohanim. Then Jesus says to the Pharisees, "But I say unto you, that in this place is one greater than the temple. But if ye had known what this meaneth, I will have mercy, and not sacrifice, ye would not have condemned the guiltless. For the Son of man is Lord even of the sabbath day." The traditional theological interpretation of this is that Jesus, who was God, nullified the ordinance of work on the Sabbath, since one greater than the temple was there and the Son of man is Lord even of the Sabbath day.

The Greek word which is translated "one" in the verse, *That in this place is one greater than the temple*, is in the neuter tense (the Greek reads μεῖζόν, not μεῖζός), so it should read "in this place is something greater than the temple." This literal translation alters the meaning of the text, so that there is *something* greater than the temple, not *someone*. What is the thing that is greater than the temple?

To find the answer, we must go back to the Talmud and the interpretation of the Torah that came about during the Maccabean revolt against the Seleucid Greeks, who had come up with a clever scheme to attack the Jews on the Sabbath when they would not fight back. In this story, which Jesus tells to defend his actions, David is on the run from Saul, who is trying to have David killed. David is fleeing for his life and is hungry, so the priest Ahimelech gives him the showbread to eat. According to Matthew 11:20–24, Jesus has just finished telling the cities that he was teaching in (Chorazin, Bethsaida, and Capernaum) that their inhabitants are all going to hell (cf. Matthew 11:21–23). This is not the way to make friends and influence people, and the ire of the inhabitants of these cities is (no doubt) why Jesus and his disciples are running away through grain fields rather than along the roads.

The verse "I will have mercy, and not sacrifice" from Hosea 6:6 ("For I desire kindness, not sacrifice") is what Jesus is talking about. *Mercy* was the thing that is greater than the temple. Jesus is not doing away with the Sabbath at all; he is merely giving an explanation as to why he and his disciples are violating the Sabbath ordinance against reaping grain. It is simply a case of Jesus giving his interpretation of *halacha*, not trying to abrogate the Law of the Torah. As a matter of fact, this very argument comes up in the Talmud, that all of the commandments of the Torah (with the exceptions of idolatry, murder, and incest, cf.

and his disciples were an hungered, and began to pluck the ears of corn, and to eat. 2. But when the Pharisees Saw it, they said unto him, Behold, thy disciples do that which is not lawful to do upon the sabbath day. 3. But he said unto them, Have ye not read what David did, when he was an hungred, and they that were with him; 4. How he entered into the house of God, and did eat the shewbread, which was not lawful for him to eat, neither for them which were with him, but only for the priests? 5. Or have ye not read in the law, how that on the sabbath days the priests in the temple profane the sabbath, and are blameless? 6. But I say unto you, That in this place is one greater than the temple. 7. But if ye had known what this meaneth, I will have mercy, and not sacrifice, ye would not have condemned the guiltless. 8. For the Son of man is Lord even of the sabbath day. 9. And when he was departed thence, he went into their synagogue: 10. And, behold, there was a man which had his hand withered. And they asked him, saying, Is it lawful to heal on the sabbath days? that they might accuse him. 11. And he said unto them, What man shall there be among you, that shall have one sheep, and if it fall into a pit on the sabbath day, will he not lay hold on it, and lift it out? 12. How much then is a man better than a sheep? Wherefore it is lawful to do well on the sabbath days. 13. Then saith he to the man, Stretch forth thine hand. And he stretched it forth; and it was restored whole, like as the other. 14. Then the Pharisees went out, and held a council against him, how they might destroy him. 15. But when Jesus knew it, he withdrew himself from thence: and great multitudes followed him, and he

---

Sanhedrin 74a), including reaping on the Sabbath, can in fact be laid aside in times of extreme personal danger. The example from Scripture the Talmud uses for this ruling is none other than the story of David eating the showbread when he is eluding Saul (*Menahot* 96a).

However, for Christian theologians to show that Jesus was giving a Talmudic explanation for violating the Sabbath Laws would undermine the highly important theological teaching of Jesus "doing away with the Law," which is supported by the "proof text" of Matthew 12:1–8. Even when Jesus says *the Son of man is lord of the Sabbath*, this is, in fact, a Pharisee maxim (cf. *Yoma* 85b). This in itself shows Jesus's familiarity with the Oral Law. It also shows that, far from "doing away with the Torah," he is in fact using the Oral Law, the "traditions of the scribes and the elders" as he often called them, to prove his point.

healed them all; 16. And charged them that they should not make him known: 17. That it might be fulfilled which was spoken by Esaias[2] the prophet, saying, 18. Behold my servant,[3] Whom I have chosen; my beloved, in whom my soul is well pleased: I will put my spirit upon him, and he shall shew judgment to the Gentiles. 19. He shall not strive, nor cry;[4] neither shall any man hear his voice in the streets. 20. A bruised reed shall he not break, and smoking flax shall he not quench, till he send forth judgment unto victory. 21. And in his name shall the Gentiles trust. 22. Then was

---

[2] *17. That it might be fulfilled which was spoken by Esaias.* In the *Tanach*, this quotation from Isaiah 42:1–4 reads, "Behold My servant, whom I shall uphold; My chosen one, whom My soul desired; I have placed My spirit upon him so he can bring forth justice to the nations. He will not shout nor raise his voice, nor make his voice heard in the street. He will not break (even) a bruised reed nor extinguish even flickering flax; but he will administer justice in truth. He will not slacken nor tire until he sets justice in the land and islands will long for his teaching."

The version in Matthew does not accord with this quote from the Masoritic text or from the Septuagint. In Josephus's *Antiquities of the Jews*, book 12, chapter 2, he writes that the Jews translated into Greek the "Laws of the Jews," i.e., the Torah. There is evidence that the *Tanach* proper was not translated; indeed, the Septuagint was possibly written by the church. Indeed, some see Origen himself as the author of the Septuagint. In any case, there are neither copies nor mention of any Greek translations of the Tanach (other than the Torah) before the Christian era, so it is quite possible, indeed probable, that the church produced the Septuagint, its authors altering the text at their whim as they did the text of the New Testament. This passage from the Tanach, like other passages in the New Testament that are not in accord with either the Hebrew Masoritic text or the Septuagint, probably predate the church's Septuagint, which would later become the "official" Old Testament. There are places where the New Testament Greek texts are nearly identical; for example, in Matthew 3:3, Mark 1:3, and Luke 3:4, the quotation is different from both the Masoritic text and the Greek Septuagint (cf. commentary to Matthew 9:5). Also compare the unusual terms used in Matthew 9:1–17, Mark 2:1–22, and Luke 5:17–39 with the transitional phrases in Matthew 8:16, Mark 1:32, and Luke 4:40, and Matthew 19:13, Mark 10:13, and Luke 18:15.

[3] *18. Behold my servant.* Identified as the Messiah in the *Targum* (Onkelos).

[4] *19. He shall not strive, nor cry.* Radak taught that the Messiah will not have to speak loudly nor demonstrate his power, and he will be accepted by all men. Despite repeated attempts to demonstrate his power, Jesus was not even accepted by the majority of his own people.

brought unto him one possessed with a devil, blind, and dumb: and he healed him, insomuch that the blind and dumb both spake and saw. 23. And all the people were amazed, and said, Is not this the son of David? 24. But when the Pharisees heard it, they said, This fellow doth not cast out devils, but by Beelzebub the prince of the devils. 25. And Jesus knew their thoughts, and said unto them, Every kingdom divided against itself is brought to desolation; and every city or house divided against itself shall not stand: 26. And if Satan cast out Satan, he is divided against himself; how shall then his kingdom stand? 27. And if I by Beelzebub cast out devils, by whom do your children cast them out? therefore they shall be your judges. 28. But if I cast out devils by the Spirit of God, then the kingdom of God is come unto you.[5] 29. Or else how can one enter into a strong man's house, and spoil his goods, except he first bind the strong man? and then he will spoil his house.[6] 30. He that is not with me is against me; and he that gathereth not with me scattereth abroad. 31. Wherefore I say unto you, All manner of sin and blasphemy shall be forgiven unto men: but the blasphemy against the Holy Ghost shall not be forgiven unto men. 32. And whosoever speaketh a word against the Son of man, it shall be forgiven him:[7] but whosoever speaketh against the Holy Ghost, it shall not be forgiven him, neither in this world, neither in the world to come.[8]

---

[5] 28. *then the kingdom of God is come unto you.* The Messianic kingdom. Cf. commentary to verse 38.

[6] 29. *then he will spoil his house.* Here Jesus teaches by giving an example of how to commit larceny.

[7] 32. *And whosoever speaketh a word against the Son of man, it shall be forgiven him.* According to Jesus, believing that he was not the Messiah is not an unforgivable sin. Matthew also changes Mark 3:28 from "sons of men" to "Son of Man."

[8] 32. *neither in the world to come.* Although this can be understood as a violation of the prohibition of blasphemy, it is also the basis for the Christian teaching that correct theology is more important than correct actions. In their monomaniacal quest for personal "salvation" (one of the hallmarks of Gnosticism), Christians teach that God is more concerned with your relationship with Him than He is with your relationship with your fellow man, and that your "divine service" (such as prayer, worship, etc.) is of greater importance than social justice (although, according to Christian theology, you still get heavenly "brownie-points"

33. *Either make the tree good, and his fruit good; or else make the*

for being nice to others).

Many Noahides who have come out of Christianity—even if they are no longer idolaters—still make this fundamental mistake of thinking that the "religious" aspects of the Torah (such as organized and written prayers, keeping Jewish holidays and festivals such as Shabbat and Sukkot, wearing Noahide prayer shawls, and the like) are more important than the "mundane" aspects of the Seven Laws that deal with one's relationship with their fellow man, such as theft or courts of law. This point of view is neither Torah-true Jewish nor Torah-true Noahide. As Rabbi Adin Steinsaltz explains in his commentary on the Talmud, "The Torah makes no essential distinction between 'matters between a man and his Creator' (דברים שבין אדם למקום) and those 'between man and his fellowman' (דברים שבין אדם לחברו), because the structure of relationships between human beings is intimately connected to the relationship between man and his Creator" (*Bava Metzia*, Vol. 1, New York: Random House, 1989, 1–2). To think that it is more pleasing to God when we engage in group prayer and worship than making sure we do not cheat, rob, or defraud our fellow man is a Christian concept, not a Jewish one. When the Talmud teaches that "Rabbi Meir ... [taught] that even an idolater who engrosses himself in Torah study is like a Kohen Gadol," too many Noahides miss the next line: "[This] refers to their Seven Noahide Commandments" (*Sanhedrin* 59a, *Shottenstein Talmud Bavli*, Brooklyn: Mesorah Publications, Ltd., 2004). Even if the study of Torah leads a Noahide to the study of most of the 613 mitzvot, it is only to better understand the Seven Laws that were given to him or her to observe. As the Talmud teaches, "he who is commanded and does stands higher than he who is not commanded and does" (*Avoda Zarah*, 3a).

Three examples from the *Tanach* illustrate the importance of the Noahide's relationship to his fellow man. The Flood of Noah was decreed because of the violation of the Noahide law of theft, not because the generation of the Flood lacked the proper written prayers: "The decree of the Flood was sealed, precluding the possibility of salvation for individuals, due to the sin of robbery" (Commentary to *Sanhedrin* 108a, *Schottenstein Talmud, Talmud Bavli*). Likewise, the people of Sodom were destroyed because of their selfishness and a lack of charity, not because their group worship was deemed insufficient: "Sodom was concerned in protecting what it had and in not sharing it with others ... [i]n the eyes of God, the greatest abomination of all is a social contract founded on selfishness" (*Bereishis*, Brooklyn: Mesorah Publications, Ltd., 2002, 596). The people of Sodom lived by the principle of "what is mine is mine and what is yours is yours," a principle which denotes a wicked attitude, the sort of non-Jewish attitude popularized by the philosophy of the apostate Ayn Rand.

The last and most striking example is the sin of the Ninevites. God sent the prophet Yonah to get the Ninevites to repent, not because they ignored the Sabbath candle-lighting and prayers, but from the violation of the sin of theft: "Radak explains that the sin of the Ninevites lay especially in the area of חמס,

tree corrupt, and his fruit corrupt: for the tree is known by his fruit. 34. O generation of vipers, how can ye, being evil, speak good things?[9] *for out of the abundance of the heart the mouth speaketh. 35. A good man out of the good treasure of the heart bringeth forth good things: and an evil man out of the good treasure of the heart*

---

robbery and *oppression* ... [t]hus it paralleled the evil of the Generation of the Deluge ... [as well as] the Sodomites. As a general rule, God intervenes directly in the affairs of the nations only when they resort to this form of behavior because it is destructive of the social order and, therefore, contrary to His wish that man live and thrive in a society" (*Yonah*, Brooklyn: Mesorah Publications Ltd., 1988, 81). Both *Abarbanel* and *Malbim* point out that, although the Ninevites were idolaters, it was only the sin of *theft* that they were required to repent for to save themselves from destruction, and this view is directly opposed to the Christian teaching that correct theology is more important than correct behavior.

This is not to diminish the importance of the law of idolatry; after all, the belief in One God, the God of Abraham, Isaac, and Jacob, is the foundation of the Torah for both Jews and Noahides. What needs to be pointed out is that the Noahide should be more concerned with what *God* thinks is important instead of what *man* thinks is important. In this case, it is understanding the proper service of the B'nai Noah in regard to keeping the Seven Laws instead of creating a "Noahide religion" based on religious elements that they were not commanded to do, such as organized prayer and worship, wearing *tzitit*, and keeping the Jewish Sabbath. This is the Christian belief, that committing the sin of blasphemy—the sin against the Holy Spirit—is more important than committing sins against his fellow man. For the Noahide, there should be no distinction: both are equally important. Concentrating on communal worship and having organized prayer and keeping Jewish holidays *at the expense of observing the laws of theft and social justice* is simply fulfilling the desire for organized religion (and it should be emphasized that organized religion is prohibited to the Noahide). Prayer and worship are indeed important, and a Noahide can and should pray to *HaShem* (cf. the note to Matthew 6:8, above), but the Noahide needs to focus on the obligation to fulfill the Seven Laws before taking on extra laws that were not commanded them. As Rabbi Matis Roberts has written, "Do not think that the sacrifices you offer ... will suffice to ward off My retribution for your deeds. For I seek from you benevolence in your dealings with each other, as well as knowledge of Me and fidelity to My statues, not merely the ritual acts of bringing sacrifices (Abarbanel) ... This follows the translation of Targum as well. Radak interprets *knowledge of God* to refer to the following of His ways, which is a further reference to human interaction" (*Trei Asar*, Brooklyn: Mesorah Publications, Ltd., 1995, 62).

[9] 34. *O generation of vipers, how can ye, being evil, speak good things.* Jesus again slanders the Pharisees.

bringeth forth good things: and an evil man out of the evil treasure bringeth forth evil things. 36. But I say unto you, That every idle word that men shall speak, they shall give account thereof in the day of judgment. 37. For by thy words thou shalt be justified, and by thy words thou shalt be condemned. 38. Then certain of the scribes and of the Pharisees answered, saying, Master, we would see a sign from thee.[10] *39. But he answered and said unto them, An evil and adulterous generation seeketh after a sign; and there shall no sign be given to it,*[11] *but the sign of the prophet Jonas: 40. For as Jonas was three days and three nights in the whale's belly;*[12] *so shall the Son of man be three days and three nights in the heart of the Earth.*[13] *41. The men of Nineveh shall rise in judgment with this generation, and shall condemn it: because they repented at the preaching of Jonas; and, behold, a greater than Jonas is here. 42. The queen of the south shall rise up in the judgment with this generation, and shall condemn it: for she came from the uttermost parts of the earth to hear the wisdom of Solomon; and, behold, a greater than Solomon is here. 43. When the unclean spirit is gone out of a man, he walketh through dry places, seeking rest, and*

---

[10] 38. *we would see a sign from thee.* The Jews are not asking to see a magic show, but for Jesus to prove his messianic claims as the Torah commands in Deuteronomy 18:15–22. (cf. *Sanhedrin* 89a). Just two verses later, Jesus gives a false prophecy that negates his claim of being the Messiah.

[11] 39. *no sign be given to it.* When asked to give a sign that he was the Messiah, Jesus always refused. To proclaim himself as a prophet, yet not show the required sign, as God commanded in the Torah, was punishable by death. "But the prophet who willfully shall speak a word in My name, that which I have not commanded him to speak … that prophet shall die" (Deuteronomy 18:20).

[12] 40. *For as Jonas was three days and three nights in the whale's belly.* Three days and three nights is not in agreement in any way with the resurrection account, for Jesus was crucified on Friday, and "resurrected" early Sunday, i.e., after sunset on Saturday (by Jewish standards of measuring time), a mere thirty or so hours (cf. Matt. 28:1).

[13] 40. *so shall the Son of man be three days and three nights in the heart of the earth.* The text in the Gospel of the Nazaraeans does not have the words "three days and three nights." A recently discovered three-foot tablet written in Hebrew that has been dated to several decades before Jesus was born suggests that there was a tradition in Judaism of a Messiah who would rise from the dead after three days.

findeth none. 44. Then he saith, I will return into my house from whence I came out; and when he is come, he findeth it empty, swept, and garnished. 45. Then goeth he, and taketh with himself seven other spirits more wicked than himself, and they enter in and dwell there: and the last state of that man is worse than the first. Even so shall it be also unto this wicked generation. 46. While he yet talked to the people, behold, his mother and his brethren stood without, desiring to speak with him. 47. Then one said unto him, Behold, thy mother and thy brethren stand without, desiring to speak with thee.[14] *48. But he answered and said unto him that told him, Who is my mother? and who are my brethren? 49. And he stretched forth his hand toward his disciples, and said, Behold my mother and my brethren!*[15] *50. For whosoever shall do the will of my Father*[16] *which is in heaven, the same is my brother, and sister, and mother.*

---

[14] *47. Then one said unto him, Behold, thy mother and thy brethren stand without, desiring to speak with thee.* Several important early witnesses omit this verse, including Codices Sinaiticus and Vaticanus.

[15] *49. And he stretched forth his hand toward his disciples, and said, Behold my mother and my brethren!* This can only be viewed as disrespect on the part of Jesus toward his mother.

[16] *50. For whosoever shall do the will of my Father.* The "will" of the Father is the Torah. It seems odd that Jesus would only consider those who kept the Torah his "mother and his brethren" when Christians teach that he came to do away with the Law.

XIII

1. The same day went Jesus out of the house, and sat by the sea side. 2. And great multitudes were gathered together unto him, so that he went into a ship, and sat; and the whole multitude stood on the shore. 3. And he spake many things unto them in parables, saying, Behold, a sower went forth to sow; 4. And when he sowed, some seeds fell by the way side, and the fowls came and devoured them up: 5. Some fell upon stony places, where they had not much earth: and forthwith they sprung up, because they had no deepness of earth: 6. And when the sun was up, they were scorched; and because they had no root, they withered away. 7. And some fell among thorns;[1] and the thorns sprung up, and choked them: 8. But other fell into good ground, and brought forth fruit, some an hundredfold, some sixtyfold, some thirtyfold. 9. Who hath ears to hear, let him hear.[2] 10. And the disciples came, and said unto him, Why speakest thou unto them in parables? 11. He answered and said unto them, Because it is given unto you to know the mysteries of the kingdom of heaven, but to them it is not given.[3] 12. For whosoever hath, to him shall be given, and he shall have more abundance: but whosoever hath not, from him shall be taken away even that he hath. 13. Therefore speak I to them in parables: because they seeing see not; and hearing they hear not, neither do they understand. 14. And in them is fulfilled the prophecy of Esaias, which saith, By hearing ye shall hear, and shall not understand; and seeing ye shall see, and shall not perceive: 15. For this people's

---

[1] 13:7. *And some fell among thorns.* Cf. Jeremiah 12:13: *They sowed wheat but reaped thorns.*

[2] 9. *Who hath ears to hear, let him hear.* Several early texts have *Let anyone with ears listen*, and other Greek manuscripts have *Let anyone with ears to hear listen.*

[3] 11. *He answered and said unto them, Because it is given unto you to know the mysteries of the kingdom of heaven, but to them it is not given.* Cf. Clement of Alexandria, *Miscellanies* V.10:63, 7: "Not grudgingly did the Lord declare in a certain gospel, *'My secret is for me and the offspring of my house.'"* Here is Jesus instructing about mystery and secret teachings, teachings that can only be described as Gnostic.

heart is waxed gross, and their ears are dull of hearing, and their eyes they have closed; lest at any time they should see with their eyes, and hear with their ears, and should understand with their heart, and should be converted, and I should heal them. 16. But blessed are your eyes, for they see: and your ears, for they hear. 17. For verily I say unto you, That many prophets and righteous men have desired to see those things which ye see, and have not seen them; and to hear those things which ye hear, and have not heard them.[4] 18. Hear ye therefore the parable of the sower. 19. When any one heareth the word of the kingdom, and understandeth it not, then cometh the wicked one, and catcheth away that which was sown in his heart. This is he which received seed by the way side. 20. But he that received the seed into stony places, the same is he that heareth the word, and anon with joy receiveth it; 21. Yet hath he not root in himself, but dureth for a while: for when tribulation or persecution ariseth because of the word, by and by he is offended. 22. He also that received seed among the thorns is he that heareth the word; and the care of this world, and the deceitfulness of riches, choke the word, and he becometh unfruitful. 23. But he that received seed into the good ground is he that heareth the word, and understandeth it; which also beareth fruit, and bringeth forth, some an hundredfold, some sixty, some thirty. 24. Another parable put he forth unto them, saying, The kingdom of heaven is likened unto a man which sowed good seed in his field: 25. But while men slept, his enemy came and sowed tares among the wheat, and went his way. 26. But when the blade was sprung up, and brought forth fruit, then appeared the tares also. 27. So the servants of the householder came and said unto him, Sir, didst not thou sow good seed in thy field? from whence then hath it tares? 28. He said unto them, An enemy hath done this. The servants said unto him, Wilt thou then that we go and gather them up? 29. But he said, Nay; lest while ye gather up the tares, ye root up also the wheat with them. 30. Let both grow together until the harvest: and in the time of harvest I will say to the reapers, Gather ye together

---

[4] 17. *and have not heard them.* This is the teaching of the Hellenistic Gnostic Christians, who said that Jesus brought a secret teaching down from heaven that no one, not even the prophets, had heard before.

first the tares, and bind them in bundles to burn them: but gather the wheat into my barn. 31. Another parable put he forth unto them, saying, The kingdom of heaven is like to a grain of mustard seed, which a man took, and sowed in his field: 32. Which indeed is the least of all seeds: but when it is grown, it is the greatest among herbs, and becometh a tree, so that the birds of the air come and lodge in the branches thereof. 33. Another parable spake he unto them; The kingdom of heaven is like unto leaven, which a woman took, and hid in three measures of meal, till the whole was leavened. 34. All these things spake Jesus unto the multitude in parables; and without a parable spake he not unto them: 35. That it might be fulfilled which was spoken by the prophet,[5] saying, I will open my mouth in parables;[6] I will utter things which have been kept secret from the foundation of the world.[7] 36. Then Jesus sent the multitude away, and went into the house: and his disciples came unto him, saying, Declare unto us the parable of the tares of the field. 37. He answered and said unto them, He that soweth the good seed is the Son of man; 38. The field is the world; the good

---

[5] 35. *spoken by the prophet.* Many early Greek manuscripts have "This was to fulfill what had been spoken through the prophet," and a few others, such as Codex Sinaiticus, have "the prophet Isaiah." This is another insertion of a "prophesy." It should be noted that this passage is from the Psalms (Psalm 78:2), not Isaiah.

[6] 35. *I will open my mouth in parables.* Cf. "Give ear, my nation, to my Torah; Bend your ear to the words of my mouth. I will open my mouth with a parable, I will utter riddles from ancient times" (Psalm 78:1–2). The first verse of this psalm contains the theme, "Give ear to the Torah!" The Torah is itself a parable (*Rashi*). If you understand the context of the psalm, then the interpretation of Jesus's parable would be that the "word of the kingdom" (v. 19) is the Torah. Anything else, such as Gnostic theology, would be heresy.

[7] 35. *things which have been kept secret from the foundation of the world.* Even in Matthew, the most "Jewish" of the gospels, there are obvious examples of Gnostic teachings. The concept of knowledge "kept secret from the foundation of the world" is one of these Gnostic concepts. Another is the parable of the hidden treasure in verse 44. In Gnosticism, the secrets of the "kingdom" were hidden from the world from the beginning and only revealed by Jesus who "came down" from heaven with this "knowledge," transmitting it by parables. The Gnostics taught that, without the "gnosis" of the secret teachings, one could not achieve salvation.

seed are the children of the kingdom; but the tares are the children of the wicked one; 39. The enemy that sowed them is the devil; the harvest is the end of the world; and the reapers are the angels. 40. As therefore the tares are gathered and burned in the fire; so shall it be in the end of this world. 41. The Son of man shall send forth his angels, and they shall gather out of his kingdom all things that offend, and them which do iniquity;[8] 42. And shall cast them into a furnace of fire: there shall be wailing and gnashing of teeth. 43. Then shall the righteous shine forth as the sun in the kingdom of their Father. Who hath ears to hear, let him hear. 44. Again, the kingdom of heaven is like unto treasure hid in a field; the which when a man hath found, he hideth, and for joy thereof goeth and selleth all that he hath, and buyeth that field. 45. Again, the kingdom of heaven is like unto a merchant man, seeking goodly pearls: 46. Who, when he had found one pearl of great price, went and sold all that he had, and bought it. 47. Again, the kingdom of heaven is like unto a net, that was cast into the sea, and gathered of every kind: 48. Which, when it was full, they drew to shore, and sat down, and gathered the good into vessels, but cast the bad away.[9] 49. So shall it be at the end of the world: the angels shall come forth, and sever the wicked from among the just,[10] 50. And shall cast them into the furnace of fire: there shall be wailing and gnashing of teeth. 51. Jesus saith unto them, Have ye understood all these things? They say unto him, Yea, Lord. 52. Then said he unto them, Therefore every scribe which is instructed unto the kingdom of heaven is like unto a man that is an householder, which bringeth

---

[8] 41. *and them which do iniquity.* The Greek word used here for "iniquity" is ἀνομίαν, which means "against the Jewish Law."

[9] 48. *gathered the good into vessels, but cast the bad away.* This is the Parable of the Kosher Fish. Only fish with fins and scales are kosher. Likewise, only "kosher" Jews will be allowed into the "kingdom of heaven" (Lev. 11:9, Deut. 14:10).

[10] 49. *the wicked from among the just.* According to Christian theology, the "wicked" are those who do not call Jesus "lord" even if they keep the Torah. For Jews, observant Noahides, and even according to Jesus himself (cf. Matthew 7:21–23), the "wicked" are those who do not keep the Torah, even if they call Jesus "lord". Which viewpoint is correct depends on how one interprets the Bible.

forth out of his treasure things new and old. 53. And it came to pass, that when Jesus had finished these parables, he departed thence. 54. And when he was come into his own country, he taught them in their synagogue, insomuch that they were astonished, and said, Whence hath this man this wisdom, and these mighty works? 55. Is not this the carpenter's son?[11] *is not his mother called Mary? and his brethren, James, and Joses, and Simon, and Judas? 56. And his sisters, are they not all with us? Whence then hath this man all these things? 57. And they were offended in him. But Jesus said unto them, A prophet is not without honour, save in his own country, and in his own house. 58. And he did not many mighty works there because of their unbelief.*

---

[11] 55. *Is not this the carpenter's son?* Jesus was Joseph's biological son (cf. note to Matthew 1:16).

XIV

1. At that time Herod the tetrarch heard of the fame of Jesus, 2. And said unto his servants, This is John the Baptist; he is risen from the dead; and therefore mighty works do shew forth themselves in him. 3. For Herod had laid hold on John, and bound him, and put him in prison for Herodias' sake, his brother Philip's wife.[1] 4. For John said unto him, It is not lawful for thee to have her. 5. And when he would have put him to death, he feared the multitude, because they counted him as a prophet. 6. But when Herod's birthday was kept, the daughter of Herodias danced before them, and pleased Herod. 7. Whereupon he promised with an oath to give her whatsoever she would ask. 8. And she, being before instructed of her mother, said, Give me here John Baptist's head in a charger. 9. And the king was sorry: nevertheless for the oath's sake, and them which sat with him at meat, he commanded it to be given her. 10. And he sent, and beheaded John in the prison. 11. And his head was brought in a charger, and given to the damsel: and she brought it to her mother. 12. And his disciples came, and took up the body, and buried it, and went and told Jesus. 13. When Jesus heard of it, he departed thence by ship into a desert place apart: and when the people had heard thereof, they followed him on foot out of the cities. 14. And Jesus went forth, and saw a great multitude, and was moved with compassion toward them, and he healed their sick. 15. And when it was evening, his disciples came to him, saying, This is a desert place, and the time is now past; send the multitude away, that they may go into the villages, and buy themselves victuals. 16. But Jesus said unto them, They need not depart; give ye them to eat. 17. And they say unto him, We have here but five loaves, and two fishes. 18. He said, Bring them hither to me. 19. And he commanded the multitude to sit down on the grass, and took the five loaves, and the two fishes, and looking up to heaven, he blessed, and brake, and gave the loaves to his disciples, and the disciples to the multitude.

---

[1] 14:3. *his brother Philip's wife.* Some of the Western texts (Bezae, Old Latin) have "his brother's wife."

20. *And they did all eat, and were filled:*[2] *and they took up of the fragments that remained twelve baskets full. 21. And they that had eaten were about five thousand men, beside women and children. 22. And straightway Jesus constrained his disciples to get into a ship, and to go before him unto the other side, while he sent the multitudes away. 23. And when he had sent the multitudes away, he went up into a mountain apart to pray: and when the evening was come, he was there alone. 24. But the ship was now in the midst of the sea, tossed with waves: for the wind was contrary.*[3] *25. And in the fourth watch of the night Jesus went unto them, walking on the sea. 26. And when the disciples saw him walking on the sea, they were troubled, saying, It is a spirit; and they cried out for fear. 27. But straightway Jesus spake unto them, saying, Be of good cheer; it is I;*[4] *be not afraid. 28. And Peter answered him and said, Lord, if it be thou, bid me come unto thee on the water. 29. And he said, Come. And when Peter was come down out of the ship, he walked on the water, to go to Jesus. 30. But when he saw the wind boisterous,*[5] *he was afraid; and beginning to sink, he cried, saying, Lord, save me. 31. And immediately Jesus stretched forth his hand, and caught him, and said unto him, O thou of little*

---

[2] 20. *And they did all eat, and were filled.* Cf. 2 Kings 4:42–44, where Elisha had already performed this miracle of feeding the multitude with a few loaves.

[3] 24. *But the ship was now in the midst of the sea, tossed with waves: for the wind was contrary.* Many early Greek texts have *but by this time the boat, battered by the waves, was far from the land, for the wind was against them.* Others omit *far distant from the land and instead have was out on the sea.*
> *but by this time the boat, battered by the waves, was far from the land, for the wind was against them*: B, Θ, φ, sy^c, sy^p, sa, bo
> Omit *far distant from the land, and insert, was out on the sea*: 𝕂, ℵ, C, D, W, λ, it, vg

[4] 27. *it is I.* ἐγώ εἰμι; the same words Jesus used in John 8:58. Cf. Matthew 24:5.

[5] 30. *the wind boisterous.* The word ἰσχυρόν ("boisterous") is in Sinaiticus and Vaticanus, but is not found in the newer versions of the New Testament that are based on these texts (the translation committees said it sounded "too Egyptian," i.e., too "Alexandrian"). Here is a modern committee of Christian Bible scholars deciding what words to leave out of the English translation, even though they are backed up in the ancient texts.

faith, wherefore didst thou doubt? 32. And when they were come into the ship, the wind ceased. 33. Then they that were in the ship came and worshipped him, saying, Of a truth thou art the Son of God. 34. And when they were gone over, they came into the land of Gennesaret. 35. And when the men of that place had knowledge of him, they sent out into all that country round about, and brought unto him all that were diseased; 36. And besought him that they might only touch the hem of his garment: and as many as touched were made perfectly whole.

XV

1. Then came to Jesus scribes and Pharisees, which were of Jerusalem, saying, 2. Why do thy disciples transgress the tradition of the elders?[1] for they wash not their hands when they eat bread. 3. But he answered and said unto them,[2] Why do ye also transgress the commandment of God by your tradition? 4. For God commanded, saying, Honour thy father and mother:[3] and, He that curseth father or mother, let him die the death. 5. But ye say, Whosoever shall say to his father or his mother, It is a gift, by whatsoever thou mightest be profited by me; 6. And honour not his father or his mother, he shall be free. Thus have ye made the commandment of God of none effect by your tradition. 7. Ye hypocrites, well did Esaias prophesy of you, saying, 8. This people draweth nigh unto me with their mouth, and honoureth me with their lips; but their heart is far from me. 9. But in vain they do worship me,[4] teaching for doctrines the commandments of men.

---

[1] *15:2. Why do thy disciples transgress the tradition of the elders?* Cf. Mark 7:1–23. The Pharisees, seeing Jesus's followers disobeying *halacha*, ask him why.

[2] *3. But he answered and said unto them.* Instead of answering their perfectly legitimate question as to why his disciples do not keep the Law, Jesus reacts with hostility, pointing an accusing finger at the Pharisees.

[3] *4. Honour thy father and mother.* Jesus accuses the Pharisees of something of which he himself is guilty—dishonoring his parents—as seen in Luke 2:48–49 and Matthew 12:46–49.

[4] *9. But in vain they do worship me.* In the King James Bible, this quote from Isaiah 29:13 reads, "Wherefore the Lord said, Forasmuch as this people draw near me with their mouth, and with their lips do honour me, but have removed their heart far from me, and their fear toward me is taught by the precept of men." This passage has, for centuries, been used against the Jewish people, describing them as pettifogging legalists who dishonor God with their nitpicking attention to the Law rather than "spiritual" matters, which means accepting the "love of Christ."

The last verses of this same chapter in Isaiah from the *Stone Tanach*, however, put the above verse in its proper context: "For the fierce man is no more and the scoffer has ceased to be; and all who strive for iniquity will be cut off: those who with a word cause man to sin and ensnare the one who gives rebuke at the city gate, and mislead the righteous with falsehood. Therefore, thus said *HaShem*, Who redeemed Abraham, to the House of Jacob: Jacob will not be

10. And he called the multitude, and said unto them, Hear, and understand: 11. Not that which goeth into the mouth defileth a man; but that which cometh out of the mouth, this defileth a man. 12. Then came his disciples, and said unto him, Knowest thou that the Pharisees were offended, after they heard this saying? 13. But he answered and said, Every plant, which my heavenly Father hath not planted, shall be rooted up. 14. Let them alone: they be blind leaders of the blind. And if the blind lead the blind, both shall fall into the ditch. 15. Then answered Peter and said unto him, Declare unto us this parable. 16. And Jesus said, Are ye also yet without understanding? 17. Do not ye yet understand, that whatsoever entereth in at the mouth goeth into the belly, and is cast out into the draught? 18. But those things which proceed out of the mouth come forth from the heart; and they defile the man. 19. For out of the heart proceed evil thoughts, murders, adulteries, fornications, thefts, false witness, blasphemies: 20. These are the things which defile a man: but to eat with unwashen hands defileth not a man. 21. Then Jesus went thence, and departed into the coasts of Tyre and Sidon. 22. And, behold, a woman of Canaan came out of the same coasts, and cried unto him, saying, Have mercy on me, O Lord, thou Son of David; my daughter is grievously vexed with a devil. 23. But he answered her not a word. And his disciples came and besought him, saying, Send her away; for she crieth after us. 24. But he answered and said, I am not sent but unto the lost sheep of the house of Israel.[5] 25. Then came she and worshipped

---

ashamed now, and his face will not pale now, when he sees his children, My handiwork in their mist, who will sanctify Israel! Those of misguided spirit will attain understanding, and complainers will learn [God's] instruction" (Isaiah 29:20–24). By twisting of the meaning of the text of Isaiah, Christians have taught their "traditions of men"—the non-Jewish, manmade Gnostic traditions like the trinity, the incarnation, and original sin—instead of the Torah.

[5] 24. *I am not sent but unto the lost sheep of the house of Israel* As in Matthew 10:5, Jesus says that his mission is to the Jews only. In Christian propaganda, Jesus is often portrayed as this all-loving figure who especially adores children. But here we have a distraught woman begging Jesus to help her daughter, and he brushes her off twice, saying that he was only interested in helping Jews. He also calls her a dog. Only after her third entreaty, when she prostrates herself before him, does he agree to help.

him, saying, Lord, help me. 26. But he answered and said, It is not meet to take the children's bread, and to cast it to dogs.⁶ 27. And she said, Truth, Lord: yet the dogs eat of the crumbs which fall from their masters' table. 28. Then Jesus answered and said unto her, O woman, great is thy faith: be it unto thee even as thou wilt. And her daughter was made whole from that very hour. 29. And Jesus departed from thence, and came nigh unto the sea of Galilee; and went up into a mountain, and sat down there. 30. And great multitudes came unto him, having with them those that were lame, blind, dumb, maimed, and many others, and cast them down at Jesus' feet; and he healed them: 31. Insomuch that the multitude wondered, when they saw the dumb to speak, the maimed to be whole, the lame to walk, and the blind to see: and they glorified the God of Israel. 32. Then Jesus called his disciples unto him, and said, I have compassion on the multitude, because they continue with me now three days, and have nothing to eat: and I will not send them away fasting, lest they faint in the way. 33. And his disciples say unto him, Whence should we have so much bread in the wilderness, as to fill so great a multitude? 34. And Jesus saith unto them, How many loaves have ye? And they said, Seven, and a few little fishes. 35. And he commanded the multitude to sit down on the ground. 36. And he took the seven loaves and the fishes, and gave thanks, and brake them, and gave to his disciples, and the disciples to the multitude. 37. And they did all eat, and were filled: and they took up of the broken meat that was left seven baskets full. 38. And they that did eat were four thousand men, beside women and children. 39. And he sent away the multitude, and took ship, and came into the coasts of Magdala.

---

⁶ 26. *cast it to dogs*. According to the church fathers, "dogs" referred to gentiles.

XVI

1. The Pharisees also with the Sadducees came, and tempting desired him that he would shew them a sign from heaven.[1] *2. He answered and said unto them, When it is evening, ye say, It will be fair weather: for the sky is red. 3. And in the morning, It will be foul weather to day: for the sky is red and lowering. O ye hypocrites, ye can discern the face of the sky; but can ye not discern the signs of the times?*[2] *4. A wicked and adulterous generation seeketh after*

---

[1] 16:1. *a sign from heaven*. Cf. *Rambam, Hilchot Yesodei Hatorah*, 10:1: "The sign of [the truth of his prophecy] will be the fulfillment of his prediction of future events, as [implied by Deuteronomy 18:21]: 'How shall we recognize that a prophecy was not spoken by God?' Therefore, if a person whose [progress] in the service of God makes him fit for prophecy arises [and claims to be a prophet] — if he does not intend to add [to] or diminish [the Torah], but rather to serve God through the *mitzvot* of the Torah — we do not tell him: 'Split the sear for us, revive the dead, or the like, and then we will believe in you.' Instead, we tell him, 'If you are a prophet, tell us what will happen in the future.' He makes his statements, and we wait to see whether [his 'prophecy' comes to fruition or not. Should even a minute particular of his 'prophecy' not materialize, he is surely a false prophet."

Jesus tried to base his authority on miracles alone (cf. Matt. 11:2–5). Not only were there "prophecies" that of Jesus that did not come true (e.g., Matt. 16:28, *Verily I say unto you, there be some standing here, which shall not taste of death, till they see the Son of man coming in his kingdom* and Matt. 24:34; *Verily I say unto you, This generation shall not pass, till all these things be fulfilled*) but the one "sign" that he gave—Matt. 12:39–40, *But he answered and said unto them, An evil and adulterous generation seeketh after a sign; and there shall no sign be given to it, but the sign of the prophet Jonas: For as Jonas was three days and three nights in the whale's belly; so shall the Son of man be three days and three nights in the heart of the Earth*—was also a false prophecy, since Jesus was only dead for about thirty hours or so, having died Friday afternoon and "risen" early after the Sabbath, which is to say after the sun went down the next day (early Sunday).

[2] 3. *can ye not discern the signs of the times?* The end of verse 2 and all of verse 3 are not found in either Sinaiticus or Vaticanus, the two most reliable and earliest of the Greek manuscripts that contain Matthew chapter 16.

Text: ℵ, C, D, W, Θ, λ, it, vg, sy^p, bo (some MSS.)
And in the morning, It will be foul weather to day: for the sky is red and lowring. O ye hypocrites, ye can discern the face of the sky; but can ye not discern the signs of the times?

a sign; and there shall no sign be given unto it, but the sign of the prophet Jonas. And he left them, and departed. 5. And when his disciples were come to the other side, they had forgotten to take bread. 6. Then Jesus said unto them, Take heed and beware of the leaven of the Pharisees and of the Sadducees. 7. And they reasoned among themselves, saying, It is because we have taken no bread. 8. Which when Jesus perceived, he said unto them, O ye of little faith, why reason ye among yourselves, because ye have brought no bread? 9. Do ye not yet understand, neither remember the five loaves of the five thousand, and how many baskets ye took up? 10. Neither the seven loaves of the four thousand, and how many baskets ye took up? 11. How is it that ye do not understand that I spake it not to you concerning bread, that ye should beware of the leaven of the Pharisees and of the Sadducees? 12. Then understood they how that he bade them not beware of the leaven of bread, but of the doctrine of the Pharisees and of the Sadducees.³ 13. When Jesus came into the coasts of Caesarea Philippi, he asked his disciples, saying, Whom do men say that I the Son of man am?⁴ 14. And they said, Some say that thou art John the Baptist:

---

omitted: א, B, φ, sy^c, sy^s, sa, bo (some MSS.)

³ 12. *but of the doctrine of the Pharisees and of the Sadducees.* The "doctrines" of the Pharisees and the Sadducees were quite different from one another. For example, the Sadducees did not accept the Oral Law. In this passage, Jesus refers to his "miracles" of the multiplication of the bread and fish. The words of Deuteronomy 13:2–5 come to mind: "If there should stand up in your midst a prophet or a dreamer of a dream, and he will produce to you a sign or a wonder, and the sign or the wonder comes about, of which he spoke to you, saying, 'Let us follow gods of others that you did not know and we shall worship them!' — do not hearken to the words of that prophet or to that dreamer of a dream, for HASHEM, your God, is testing you to know whether you love HASHEM, your God, will all your heart and with all your soul. HASHEM, your God, shall you follow and Him shall you fear; His commandments shall you observe and to His voice shall you hearken; Him shall you serve and to Him shall you cleave." Christianity wants people to "believe in Jesus" because of his "miracles," which the Torah explicitly warns us not to do.

⁴ 13. *Whom do men say that I the Son of man am?* Many early manuscripts have *Who do people say that the Son of Man is?* or *Who do people say that I, the Son of Man, am?* (Irenaeus also quotes it this latter way.)

Who do people say that the Son of Man is?: א, B, vg, sa, bo

*some, Elias; and others, Jeremias, or one of the prophets. 15. He saith unto them, But whom say ye that I am? 16. And Simon Peter answered and said, Thou art the Christ, the Son of the living God. 17. And Jesus answered and said unto him, Blessed art thou, Simon Barjona: for flesh and blood hath not revealed it unto thee, but my Father which is in heaven.*⁵ *18. And I say also unto thee, That thou art Peter, and upon this rock I will build my church;*⁶ *and the gates of hell shall not prevail against it. 19. And I will give unto thee the keys of the kingdom of heaven: and whatsoever thou shalt bind on earth shall be bound in heaven:*⁷ *and whatsoever thou halt loose on earth shall be loosed in heaven. 20. Then charged he his disciples that they should tell no man that he was Jesus the Christ. 21. From that time forth began Jesus*⁸ *to shew unto his disciples, how that he must go unto Jerusalem, and suffer many things of the elders and chief priests and scribes, and be killed, and be raised again the third day. 22. Then Peter took him, and began to rebuke*

Who do people say that I, the Son of Man, am?: ℵ, C, D, W, Θ, λ, φ, it, syᶜ, syˢ, syᵖ, Irenaeus

⁵ 17. *flesh and blood hath not revealed it unto thee, but my Father which is in heaven.* Gnostics teach that only through secret knowledge from heaven, that is, the spiritual knowledge as opposed to the "flesh and blood" knowledge of the material world, can a person gain salvation. This is one of the major differences between Gnostic Christianity and Torah-observant Noahides: Gnostic Christians teach that correct theology and beliefs are more important than correct action.

⁶ 18. *upon this rock I will build my church.* The Greek word for "church" here is ἐκκλησίαν, which simply means "assembly." Jesus was not starting the Christian "church." He was building a Jewish congregation based on his own peculiar teachings of the Torah.

⁷ 19. *and whatsoever thou shalt bind on earth shall be bound in heaven.* The Greek reads *has been bound in heaven*, or what is permissible under the Law, to determine *halacha*. "The technical terms used of rabbis when issuing authoritative decisions was 'binding' or 'loosing'; 'to bind' was to declare an action unlawful, and 'to loose' was to declare it lawful. Thus Rabbi Jochanan said, 'Concerning gathering wood on a feast day, the school of Shammai binds [that is, forbids] it — the school of Hillel looses [that is, permits] it.'" Metzger, *The New Testament: Its Background, Growth, and Content*, 51.

⁸ 21. *From that time forth began Jesus.* Sinaiticus, Vaticanus, and the Bohairic texts add the word *Christ*. Irenaeus and Origen omit both names.

him, saying, Be it far from thee, Lord: this shall not be unto thee. 23. But he turned, and said unto Peter, Get thee behind me, Satan:[9] thou art an offence unto me: for thou savourest not the things that be of God, but those that be of men. 24. Then said Jesus unto his disciples, If any man will come after me, let him deny himself, and take up his cross, and follow me. 25. For whosoever will save his life shall lose it: and whosoever will lose his life for my sake shall find it. 26. For what is a man profited, if he shall gain the whole world, and lose his own soul?[10] or what shall a man give in exchange for his soul? 27. For the Son of man shall come in the glory of his Father with his angels; and then he shall reward every man according to his works.[11] 28. Verily I say unto you, There be some standing here, which shall not taste of death,[12] till they see the Son of man coming in his kingdom.

---

[9] 23. *But he turned, and said unto Peter, Get thee behind me, Satan.* Peter, the first pope, is Satan.

[10] 26. *if he shall gain the whole world, and lose his own soul?* In Gnostic thought, the material world is evil. The only way to achieve salvation is for the soul to go to heaven, or the spiritual realm.

[11] 27. *he shall reward every man according to his works.* And not because of his theology.

[12] 28. *which shall not taste of death.* Another false prophecy by Jesus. (Cf. note to Matthew 12:38).

XVII

1. And after six days Jesus taketh Peter, James, and John his brother, and bringeth them up into an high mountain apart, 2. And was transfigured before them:[1] *and his face did shine as the sun, and his raiment was white as the light. 3. And, behold, there appeared unto them Moses and Elias talking with him.*[2] *4. Then answered Peter, and said unto Jesus, Lord, it is good for us to be here: if thou wilt, let us make here three tabernacles; one for thee, and one for Moses, and one for Elias. 5. While he yet spake, behold, a bright cloud overshadowed them: and behold a voice out of the cloud, which said, This is my beloved Son, in whom I am well pleased; hear ye him. 6. And when the disciples heard it, they fell on their face, and were sore afraid. 7. And Jesus came and touched them, and said, Arise, and be not afraid. 8. And when they had lifted up their eyes, they saw no man, save Jesus only. 9. And as they came down from the Mountain, Jesus charged them, saying, Tell the vision to no man, until the Son of man be risen again from the dead. 10. And his disciples asked him, saying, Why then say the scribes that Elias must first come? 11. And Jesus answered and*

---

[1] *17:2. And was transfigured before them.* As Metzger writes, "It was not easy for the Church to defend herself against Gnosticism. Certain elements in the gospel tradition itself seemed to give verisimilitude to the Gnostics' claim" (*The Canon of the New Testament*, Oxford: Clarendon Press, 1992, 78). Ehrman writes, "Both Clement of Alexandria and Origen, for example, acknowledged that Jesus' body could readily change appearance at will—a decidedly docetic notion" (Bart D. Ehrman, *The Orthodox Corruption of Scripture*, New York: Oxford University Press, 1993, 10).

[2] *3. And, behold, there appeared unto them Moses and Elias talking with him.* The Greek word used here for "appeared" is ὤφθη, meaning "envisioned," rather than the usual Greek word for "seeing," which means "using the eyes to look at." Christians have always pointed to the Resurrection as the most amazing of Jesus's "miracles" and call it "proof" of their claims of his "divinity." But they fail to look at this in context. Here we have Moses and Elijah, who had been dead for centuries, and yet here they are talking with Jesus. The "miracle" of Jesus's Resurrection pales in significance to this supposed "miracle." Why is the Resurrection stressed, while the appearance of Moses and Elijah is not? Looking at this in the context of Moses and Elijah "appearing" to Jesus, the Resurrection is not proof of anything, save that God is all-powerful.

said unto them, Elias truly shall first come, and restore all things. 12. But I say unto you, That Elias is come already, and they knew him not, but have done unto him whatsoever they listed. Likewise shall also the Son of man suffer of them. 13. Then the disciples understood that he spake unto them of John the Baptist.[3] 14. And when they were come to the multitude, there came to him a certain man, kneeling down to him, and saying, 15. Lord, have mercy on my son: for he is lunatick, and sore vexed: for ofttimes he falleth into the fire, and oft into the water. 16. And I brought him to thy disciples, and they could not cure him. 17. Then Jesus answered and said, O faithless and perverse generation, how long shall I be with you? how long shall I suffer you? bring him hither to me. 18. And Jesus rebuked the devil; and he departed out of him: and the child was cured from that very hour. 19. Then came the disciples to Jesus apart, and said, Why could not we cast him out? 20And Jesus said unto them, Because of your unbelief: for verily I say unto you, If ye have faith as a grain of mustard seed, ye shall say unto this mountain, Remove hence to yonder place; and it shall remove; and nothing shall be impossible unto you. 21. Howbeit this kind goeth not out but by prayer and fasting.[4] 22. And while they abode in Galilee,[5] Jesus said unto them, The Son of man shall be betrayed into the hands of Men: 23. And they shall kill him, and the third day he shall be raised again. And they were exceeding sorry. 24. And when they were come to Capernaum, they that received tribute money came to Peter, and said, Doth not your master pay tribute? 25. He saith, Yes. And when he was come into the house, Jesus prevented him, saying, What thinkest thou, Simon? of whom do the

---

[3] 13. *Then the disciples understood that he spake unto them of John the Baptist.* Cf. note to Matthew 11:14.

[4] 21. *Howbeit this kind goeth not out but by prayer and fasting.* Sinaiticus, Vaticanus, and other early texts omit this entire verse.

    Omit entire verse: ℵ, B, Θ, sy^c, sy^s, sa, bo
    Text: 𝕂, C, D, W, λ, φ, it, vg, sy^p, Origen. Cf. Mark 9:29.

[5] 22. *And while they abode in Galilee.* Other early Greek texts have *As they were gathering in Galilee.*

    As they were gathering in Galilee: ℵ, B, λ, it, vg
    As they were living in Galilee: 𝕂, C, D, W, Θ, φ, sy^c, sy^s, sy^p, sa, bo

kings of the earth take custom or tribute? of their own children, or of strangers? 26. Peter saith unto him, Of strangers. Jesus saith unto him, Then are the children free. 27. Notwithstanding, lest we should offend them, go thou to the sea, and cast an hook, and take up the fish that first cometh up; and when thou hast opened his mouth, thou shalt find a piece of money: that take, and give unto them for me and thee.

XVIII

1. At the same time came the disciples unto Jesus, saying, Who is the greatest in the kingdom of heaven? 2. And Jesus called a little child unto him, and set him in the midst of them, 3. And said, Verily I say unto you, Except ye be converted,[1] and become as little children, ye shall not enter into the kingdom of heaven. 4. Whosoever therefore shall humble himself as this little child, the same is greatest in the kingdom of heaven. 5. And whoso shall receive one such little child in my name receiveth me. 6. But whoso shall offend one of these little ones which believe in me, it were better for him that a millstone were hanged about his neck, and that he were drowned in the depth of the sea. 7. Woe unto the world because of offences! for it must needs be that offences come; but woe to that man by whom the offence cometh! 8. Wherefore if thy hand or thy foot offend thee, cut them off,[2] and cast them from thee: it is better for thee to enter into life halt or maimed, rather than having two hands or two feet to be cast into everlasting fire. 9. And if thine eye offend thee, pluck it out, and cast it from thee: it is better for thee to enter into life with one eye, rather than having two eyes to be cast into hell fire. 10. Take heed that ye despise not one of these little ones; for I say unto you, That in heaven their angels do always behold the face of my Father which is in heaven. 11. For the Son of man is come to save that which was lost.[3] 12.

---

[1] 18:3. *converted.* The Christian interpretation of this verse means to be converted to Christianity, a religion that did not exist during the time of Jesus.

[2] 8. *cut them off.* The Torah forbids self-mutilation for any reason (*Makkot* 21a; cf. Deut. 14:1, Lev. 19:27–28, 21:5). Jesus ignores the teaching of God, telling his followers to chop off hands and feet and to gouge out their eyes.

[3] 11. *For the Son of man is come to save that which was lost.* This verse is not found in any Greek text of Matthew before the fifth century. *Son of man:* Jesus did not use the term Messiah (Christ). He preferred to use the term "Son of man." This term occurs eighty-one times in the gospels, all of them spoken by Jesus and never by the disciples, the Jews, or the multitudes. Psalm 146:3 reads, *Do not rely on nobles, nor in a son of man who holds no salvation.* This teaches us that one should only look to God for salvation, that God is the only savior, and not any "Son of man." Isaiah 43:11: *I, only I, am HaShem, and there is no savior aside from Me.*

How think ye? if a man have an hundred sheep, and one of them be gone astray, doth he not leave the ninety and nine, and goeth into the mountains, and seeketh that which is gone astray? 13. And if so be that he find it, verily I say unto you, he rejoiceth more of that sheep, than of the ninety and nine which went not astray. 14. Even so it is not the will of your Father[4] *which is in heaven, that one of these little ones should perish. 15. Moreover if thy brother shall trespass against thee, go and tell him his fault between thee and him alone: if he shall hear thee, thou hast gained thy brother. 16. But if he will not hear thee, then take with thee one or two more, that in the mouth of two or three witnesses every word may be established. 17. And if he shall neglect to hear them,*[5] *tell it unto the the church: but if he neglect to hear the church, let him be unto thee as an heathen*[6] *man and a publican. 18. Verily I say unto you, Whatsoever ye shall bind on earth shall be bound in heaven: and*

Text: 𝕶, D, W, it, vg, sy^c, sy^p
Omit verse 11: ℵ, B, Θ, λ, φ, sy^s, sa, bo

[4] 14. *Even so it is not the will of your Father.* Many of the early Greek manuscripts have "my Father." Codex Bezae has "our Father."

Text: 𝕶, ℵ, W, λ, it, vg, sy^c, sy^p
"my": B, Θ, φ, sy^s, sa, bo
"our": D

[5] 17. *And if he shall neglect to hear them.* The verse that Jesus quotes from in Matthew 18:16 is from Deuteronomy 19:15: "A single witness shall not stand up against any man for any iniquity or for any error, regarding any sin that he may commit; according to two witnesses or according to three witnesses shall a matter be confirmed." The subject of this verse is about personal property and the Jewish courts. The Torah teaches in Deuteronomy 19:15–21 that if two witnesses bring a charge before a Jewish court, the testimony can be offset by two other witnesses who claim the testimony of the first witnesses is false. The Torah sides with the second two witnesses.

[6] 17. *but if he neglect to hear the church, let him be unto thee as an heathen.* The Greek word for "church" here is ἐκκλησία, which means "assembly" (cf. Acts 19:32 and 39). This word is usually translated as "church" in the New Testament, although it is used to describe the Jewish assembly of the synagogue as well as non-Jewish assemblies. The Greek for "heathen" is ἐθνικος, or gentile, which means the verse actually reads "if he refuses to hear, let him be like a gentile to you." This is another example of Jesus's hostility to gentiles. Gentiles were often used by Jesus as examples of depravity or incorrect behavior, yet he would also treat his fellow Jews the same way, as seen in chapter 23.

whatsoever ye shall loose on earth shall be loosed in heaven. 19. Again I say unto you, That if two of you shall agree on earth as touching any thing that they shall ask, it shall be done for them of my Father which is in heaven. 20. For where two or three are gathered together in my name, there am I in the midst of them.[7] *21. Then came Peter to him, and said, Lord, how oft shall my brother sin against me, and I forgive him? till seven times? 22. Jesus saith unto him, I say not unto thee, Until seven times: but, Until seventy times seven. 23. Therefore is the kingdom of heaven likened unto a certain king, which would take account of his servants. 24. And when he had begun to reckon, one was brought unto him, which owed him ten thousand talents.*[8] *25. But forasmuch as he had not to pay, his lord commanded him to be sold, and his wife, and children, and all that he had, and payment to be made. 26. The servant therefore fell down, and worshipped*[9] *him, saying, lord,*[10] *have patience with me, and I will pay thee all. 27. Then the lord of that servant was moved with compassion, and loosed him, and forgave him the debt. 28. But the same servant went out, and found one of his fellowservants, which owed him an hundred pence: and he laid hands on him, and took him by the throat, saying, Pay me that thou owest. 29. And his fellowservant fell down at his feet, and besought him, saying, Have patience with me, and I will pay thee all. 30. And he would not: but went and cast him into prison, till he should pay the debt. 31. So when his fellowservants saw what was done, they were very sorry, and came and told unto their lord*

---

[7] 20. *For where two or three are gathered together in my name.* Cf. Oxyrhynchus Papyrus 1, Logion 5: *Where there are two, they are not without God; and where there is one alone, I say, I am there. Raise the stone, and there you will find me; split the wood, and there I am.*

[8] 24. *ten thousand talents.* This was 30,000,000 shekels, an outrageously large sum for a king's servant to possess.

[9] 26. *worshipped.* The Greek προσεκύνει is the same word used in Matthew 15:25. It does not mean "worshiped" in the religious sense; it simply means "to prostrate oneself." (Cf. note to Matthew 2:2.)

[10] 26. *lord.* The Greek word κύριε, "lord," was added to the text. It is not found in early manuscripts, such as Vaticanus or Bezae. It was a form of respect, not "religious worship." (Cf. 2 Kings 2:15.)

all that was done. 32. Then his lord, after that he had called him, said unto him, O thou wicked servant, I forgave thee all that debt, because thou desiredst me: 33. Shouldest not thou also have had compassion on thy fellowservant, even as I had pity on thee? 34. And his lord was wroth, and delivered him to the tormentors, till he should pay all that was due unto him. 35. So likewise shall my heavenly Father do also unto you,[11] *if ye from your hearts forgive not every one his brother their trespasses.*

---

[11] 35. *So likewise shall my heavenly Father do also unto you.* In this parable, Jesus attempts to teach forgiveness. If he had stopped at contrasting the forgiveness of the king to the man who owed him ten thousand talents with the other servant who owed the servant a hundred denarii, it would have been a better lesson, but the king has the servant thrown in prison and tortured. To suggest that God will torture those who cannot pay a debt is certainly not in the spirit of the Torah. It also goes against what Jesus himself taught in Matthew 6:12, "to forgive us our debts, as we forgive our debtors."

XIX

1. And it came to pass, that when Jesus had finished these sayings, he departed from Galilee, and came into the coasts of Judaea beyond Jordan; 2. And great multitudes followed him; and he healed them there. 3. The Pharisees also came unto him, tempting him, and saying unto him, Is it lawful for a man to put away his wife for every cause? 4. And he answered and said unto them, Have ye not read, that he which made them at the beginning made them male and female, 5. And said, For this cause shall a man leave father and mother, and shall cleave to his wife: and they twain shall be one flesh? 6. Wherefore they are no more twain, but one flesh. What therefore God hath joined together, let not man put asunder. 7. They say unto him, Why did Moses then command to give a writing of divorcement, and to put her away? 8. He saith unto them, Moses[1] *because of the hardness of your hearts suffered you to put away your wives: but from the beginning it was not so. 9. And I say unto you, Whosoever shall put away his wife, except it be for fornication, and shall marry another, committeth adultery: and whoso marrieth her which is put away doth commit adultery.*[2]

---

[1] 19:8. *He saith unto them, Moses.* Cf. Deuteronomy 24:1–4. Many modern Christian "scholars" say that Moses did not write Deuteronomy, even though Jesus says he did.

[2] 9. *except it be for fornication, and shall marry another, committeth adultery.* Jesus's view on divorce is the one instance where he sides with Shammai rather than Hillel. This is a verse of doubtful origin, however, since there are many different versions of this verse. His ruling that a divorced woman cannot remarry goes against the Torah, where Leviticus 21:14 plainly states that a divorced woman is only forbidden to a Kohen Gadol, or the high priest: *A widow, a divorcee, a desecrated woman, a harlot — he shall not marry these; only a virgin of his people; for I am HaShem Who sanctifies him.*

> *except for unchastity, and marries another commits adultery*:
> 𝔎, א, W, Θ, vg, sy^s, sy^p
> *except on the ground of unchastity, and marries another, commits adultery (against her*: sy^c): D, φ, it, sy^c, sa
> *except on the ground of unchastity, makes her commit adultery*: 𝔭25?, B, λ, bo
>
> *except for unchastity, and marries another, makes* her *commit adultery*: C

10. His disciples say unto him, If the case of the man be so with his wife, it is not good to marry. 11. But he said unto them, All men cannot receive this saying, save they to whom it is given. 12. For there are some eunuchs, which were so born from their mother's womb: and there are some eunuchs, which were made eunuchs of men: and there be eunuchs, which have made themselves eunuchs for the kingdom of heaven's sake. He that is able to receive it, let him receive it. 13. Then were there brought unto him little children, that he should put his hands on them, and pray: and the disciples rebuked them. 14. But Jesus said, Suffer little children, and forbid them not, to come unto me: for of such is the kingdom of heaven. 15. And he laid his hands on them, and departed thence.[3] 16. And, behold, one came and said unto him, Good Master, what good thing shall I do, that I may have eternal life? 17. And he said unto him, Why callest thou me good? there is none good but one, that is, God:[4] but if thou wilt enter into life, keep the commandments.[5]

> Add *And whoever marries a divorced woman commits adultery*: 𝔓25, B, C, W, Θ, λ, φ, 𝕂, it (some MSS.), vg, sy^p, bo. cf. Matthew 5:32.

[3] 15. 16–24. To Matthew 19:16–24, cf. Gospel of the Nazaraeans (in Origen, *Commentary on Matthew* 15:14 in the Latin version): "And the Lord said to him. 'How can you say, I have fulfilled the law and the prophets, when it is written in the law: You shall love your neighbor as yourself; and look, many of your neighbors, children of Abraham and Sarah, are covered with filth, dying of hunger, and your house is full of many good things, none of which is given to them?'"

[4] 17. *Why callest thou me good? there is none good but one, that is, God.* Cf. Justin (Dialogue 101.2): "One is good, my Father in the heavens." Jesus clearly refutes the claim that he is God.

[5] 17. *if thou wilt enter into life, keep the commandments.* This is the teaching in the Gospel of Matthew that is not emphasized in Christianity: keeping the Torah. The present author has written, "The Christian argument against the Noahide Code is that the Seven Laws of Noah are not found in the Christian Bible, but that they are found only in the Talmud. To the Noahide, the New Testament does not belong in the Bible, since it cannot be classified as "scripture" on the same level of the *Tanach*. The Christian criticism that the Talmud is simply orally transmitted teachings and rabbinic interpretations is illogical since the New Testament itself is essentially a "Christian Talmud"—a collection of oral transmissions written down by men who did not even know how to read the original Hebrew texts, and who falsified and corrupted the teachings they were

18. He saith unto him, Which? Jesus said, Thou shalt do no murder, Thou shalt not commit adultery, Thou shalt not steal, Thou shalt not bear false witness, 19. Honour thy father and thy mother: and, Thou shalt love thy neighbour as thyself. 20. The young man saith unto him, All these things have I kept from my youth up: what lack I yet? 21. Jesus said unto him, If thou wilt be perfect, go and sell that thou hast, and give to the poor,[6] and thou shalt have treasure in heaven: and come and follow me. 22. But when the young man heard that saying, he went away sorrowful: for he had great possessions. 23. Then said Jesus unto his disciples, Verily I say unto you, That a rich man shall hardly enter into the kingdom of heaven. 24. And again I say unto you, It is easier for a camel to go through the eye of a needle, than for a rich man to enter into the kingdom of God. 25. When his disciples heard it, they were exceedingly amazed, saying, Who then can be saved? 26. But Jesus beheld them, and said unto them, With men this is impossible; but

---

transmitting" (Cecil, *The Noahide Code*, 74–75).

If we look at the teachings of Jesus, which were orally passed down for several generations before the gospels were written in the mid-second century of the Common Era as the Christian *mishna*, and the epistles of Paul as the Christian *gemara*, it is clear how the early church used Paul's interpretation of Jesus's teaching for his "faith-based" approach. This concept was first expounded by Marcion, who used ten of Paul's epistles and the gospel of Luke to create the first New Testament in the mid-second century. Marcion was the first of the Gnostics to teach Paul's "faith-based" approach, rather than the strictly "knowledge-based" approach of the other Gnostics. Paul's teachings, however, were in themselves "knowledge-based" in that his message of "faith" contained teachings that were used to interpret the gospels. "But Paul himself, obviously, also regards the Gnostic terminology as the appropriate form of expression for the Christian understanding of existence…it is especially significant that he never adduces any of the sayings of Jesus on the Torah in favor of his own teaching about Torah" (Bultmann, *Theology of the New Testament*. New York: Charles Scribner's Sons, 1951, §15, 181).

This teaching, to keep the commandments of God, is what the Tanach teaches. The teaching of Paul—to believe that the physical sacrifice of Jesus atoned for the sins of those who believe that his physical sacrifice atoned for the sins of the world—is a Gnostic teaching. It is not a teaching of the Torah.

[6] 21. *give to the poor.* Impoverishing oneself is not a Jewish teaching. Giving charity is a mitzvah, but selling everything you own and becoming dependant on others is not.

with God all things are possible. 27. Then answered Peter and said unto him, Behold, we have forsaken all, and followed thee; what shall we have therefore? 28. And Jesus said unto them, Verily I say unto you, That ye which have followed me, in the regeneration when the Son of man shall sit in the throne of his glory,[7] ye also shall sit upon twelve thrones, judging the twelve tribes of Israel. 29. And every one that hath forsaken houses, or brethren, or sisters, or father, or mother, or wife, or children, or lands, for my name's sake, shall receive an hundredfold,[8] and shall inherit everlasting life. 30. But many that are first shall be last; and the last shall be first.

---

[7] 28. *sit in the throne of his glory.* Here Jesus clearly shows that he was wanting to be the king of Israel.

[8] 29. *shall receive an hundredfold.* Texts B and sa have *manifold.*

XX

1. For the kingdom of heaven is like unto a man that is an householder, which went out early in the morning to hire labourers into his vineyard. 2. And when he had agreed with the labourers for a penny a day, he sent them into his vineyard. 3. And he went out about the third hour, and saw others standing idle in the marketplace, 4. And said unto them; Go ye also into the vineyard, and whatsoever is right I will give you. And they went their way. 5. Again he went out about the sixth and ninth hour, and did likewise. 6. And about the eleventh hour he went out, and found others standing idle, and saith unto them, Why stand ye here all the day idle? 7. They say unto him, Because no man hath hired us. He saith unto them, Go ye also into the vineyard; and whatsoever is right, that shall ye receive. 8. So when even was come, the lord of the vineyard saith unto his steward, Call the labourers, and give them their hire, beginning from the last unto the first. 9. And when they came that were hired about the eleventh hour, they received every man a penny. 10. But when the first came, they supposed that they should have received more; and they likewise received every man a penny. 11. And when they had received it, they murmured against the goodman of the house, 12. Saying, These last have wrought but one hour, and thou hast made them equal unto us, which have borne the burden and heat of the day. 13. But he answered one of them, and said, Friend, I do thee no wrong: didst not thou agree with me for a penny? 14. Take that thine is, and go thy way: I will give unto this last, even as unto thee. 15. Is it not lawful for me to do what I will with mine own? Is thine eye evil, because I am good? 16. So the last shall be first, and the first last: for many be called, but few chosen.[1] 17. And Jesus going up to Jerusalem took the twelve disciples apart in the way, and said unto them, 18. Behold, we go up to Jerusalem; and the Son of man shall be betrayed unto the chief priests and unto the scribes, and they shall condemn him to death, 19. And shall deliver him to the Gentiles to mock, and to scourge, and to crucify him: and the third day he shall rise again. 20. Then came to

---

[1] 20:16. *for many be called, but few chosen*. This phrase is absent in ℵ, B.

him the mother of Zebedee's children with her sons, worshipping him, and desiring a certain thing of him. 21. And he said unto her, What wilt thou? She saith unto him, Grant that these my two sons may sit, the one on thy right hand, and the other on the left, in thy kingdom. 22. But Jesus answered and said, Ye know not what ye ask. Are ye able to drink of the cup that I shall drink of, and to be baptized with the baptism that I am baptized with?[2] They say unto him, We are able. 23. And he saith unto them, Ye shall drink indeed of my cup, and be baptized with the baptism that I am baptized with: but to sit on my right hand, and on my left, is not mine to give, but it shall be given to them for whom it is prepared of my Father. 24. And when the ten heard it, they were moved with indignation against the two brethren. 25. But Jesus called them unto him, and said, Ye know that the princes of the Gentiles exercise dominion over them, and they that are great exercise authority upon them. 26. But it shall not be so among you: but whosoever will be great among you, let him be your minister; 27. And whosoever will be chief among you, let him be your servant: 28. Even as the Son of man came not to be ministered unto, but to minister, and to give his life a ransom for many.[3] 29. And as they departed from Jericho, a great multitude followed him. 30. And, behold, two blind men

---

[2] 22. *to be baptized with the baptism that I am baptized with?* This phrase is absent in Sinaiticus and other early manuscripts. Cf. the Gospel of the Naassenes (Hippolytus, *Refutation of All Heresies*, V.8:11): "'But' Jesus says, 'even if you drink the cup which I drink, you will not be able to enter where I go.'"

[3] 28. *and to give his life a ransom for many.* The Western texts, Bezae, φ, it, and sy^c have an expanded text after πολλῶν ("many"): "But seek to increase from that which is small, and to become less from that which is greater. When you enter into a house and are summoned to dine, do not sit down at the prominent places, lest perchance a man more honourable than you come in afterwards, and he who invited you come and say to you, 'Go down lower'; and you shall be ashamed. But if you sit down in the inferior place, and one inferior to you come in, then he that invited you will say to you, 'Go up higher'; and this will be advantageous for you This interpolation is a piece of floating tradition, an expanded bun inferior version of Lk 14:8–10" (Metzger, *The Text of the New Testament*, 1980, 50). This is an example of why the Western text, the earliest text of the New Testament known, has never been made into a popular English Bible; it would have too many verses that would be unfamiliar to Christians, leading them to doubt the veracity of the New Testament.

sitting by the way side, when they heard that Jesus passed by, cried out, saying, Have mercy on us, O Lord, thou Son of David. 31. And the multitude rebuked them, because they should hold their peace: but they cried the more, saying, Have mercy on us, O Lord, thou Son of David. 32. And Jesus stood still, and called them, and said, What will ye that I shall do unto you? 33. They say unto him, Lord, that our eyes may be opened. 34. So Jesus had compassion on them, and touched their eyes: and immediately their eyes received sight, and they followed him.

XXI

1. And when they drew nigh unto Jerusalem, and were come to Bethphage, unto the mount of Olives, then sent Jesus two disciples, 2. Saying unto them, Go into the village over against you, and straightway ye shall find an ass tied, and a colt with her: loose them, and bring them unto me. 3. And if any man say ought unto you, ye shall say, The Lord hath need of them; and straightway he will send them. 4. All this was done, that it might be fulfilled which was spoken by the prophet,[1] saying, 5. Tell ye the daughter of Sion, Behold, thy King cometh unto thee, meek, and sitting upon an ass, and a colt the foal of an ass. 6. And the disciples went, and did as Jesus commanded them, 7. And brought the ass, and the colt, and put on them their clothes,[2] and they set him thereon. 8. And a very great multitude spread their garments in the way; others cut down branches from the trees, and strawed them in the way. 9. And the multitudes that went before, and that followed,[3] cried, saying, Hosanna to the Son of David: Blessed is he that cometh in the name of the Lord;[4] Hosanna in the highest. 10. And when he was come

---

[1] *21:4. fulfilled which was spoken by the prophet.* Some witnesses (M^{mg} 42, it^a, c, h, cop^{boms}) have Ζαχαρίου (Zechariah); other witnesses (vg^{ms} cop^{pms}), who did not know where the verses came from, have "Isaiah."

[2] *7. And brought the ass, and the colt, and put on them their clothes.* Some early Western texts have "put on it" or "on the colt"; a few texts omit the phrase entirely. Most of the texts of Matthew, though, have the absurd spectacle of Jesus riding into Jerusalem on two animals at the same time, another example of the author of Matthew not understanding the text of the *Tanach*.

    Text: 𝕂, ℵ, B, C, W, λ, vg, sa, bo
    "on it": D, Θ, φ, it
    "on the colt": sy^p
    Phrase omitted: sy^c

[3] *9. And the multitudes that went before, and that followed.* This is the crowd Jesus brought with him from Jericho. Cf. Matthew 20:29, which tells us that Jesus entered Jericho with his disciples and left Jericho with a large mob of his followers. It is this mob that is proclaiming him Messiah, not the people of Jerusalem (cf. 21:10, "And when he was come into Jerusalem, all the city was moved, saying, Who is this?").

[4] *9. Blessed is he that cometh in the name of the Lord.* From Psalm 118:26: *Blessed is he who comes in the Name of HaShem.*

into Jerusalem, all the city was moved, saying, Who is this? 11. And the multitude said, This is Jesus the prophet of Nazareth of Galilee. 12. And Jesus went into the temple of God,[5] and cast out all them that sold and bought in the temple,[6] and overthrew the tables of the moneychangers, and the seats of them that sold doves, 13. And said unto them, It is written, My house shall be called the house of prayer; but ye have made it a den of thieves. 14. And the blind and the lame came to him in the temple; and he healed them. 15. And when the chief priests and scribes saw the wonderful things that he did, and the children crying in the temple, and saying, Hosanna to the Son of David; they were sore displeased, 16. And said unto him, Hearest thou what these say? And Jesus saith unto them, Yea; have ye never read, Out of the mouth of babes and sucklings thou hast perfected praise?[7] 17. And he left them, and went out of the city

---

[5] *12. And Jesus went into the temple of God.* Many of the early texts, including Sinaiticus and Vaticanus, omit the words "of God." In the Gospel of the Nazaraeans, Matthew 21:12 is quoted in a note in a thirteenth-century manuscript of the Aurora by Peter of Riga, who was obviously an X-Men comics fan: "In the Gospel books which the Nazarenes use it is written; from his eyes went forth rays which terrified them and put them to flight."
    Text: 𝕶, C, D, W, λ, it, vg, **sy**^{c}, sy^p
    Omit "of God": K, ℵ, B, Θ, φ, sa, bo

[6] *12. and cast out all them that sold and bought in the temple.* Cf. note to Matthew 26:51. Jesus and the mob he brought with him take over the temple and drive out the Sadducees. This was no doubt a more important event than the gospels make it, although there are hints (Mark 15:7, Luke 23:19, 25) that there had been an insurrection in the city. Jesus and his followers are attempting a *coup d'état* with the mob he brought with him from Jericho. Jesus was the leader of this insurrection. It led to his arrest and execution on charges of sedition.

[7] *16. Out of the mouth of babes and sucklings thou hast perfected praise?* The quotation in Matthew follows the Septuagint ("praise" instead of "strength," which is in the Masoritic text). This is a quotation of Psalm 8:3: "Out of the mouth of babes and sucklings You have established strength, because of Your tormentors: to silence foe and avenger." The meaning of the first part of the verse in Psalms tells that even infants and young children can recognize the hand of God in the world. The second part of the verse speaks of the *tsorrim* (translated in the KJV as "enemies"). As Rabbi S. R. Hirsch points out, the word *tsarar*, which is the root of *tsorrim*, means "to confine" or "to limit in space." Examples are those who would limit and confine the worship of God to certain times, places, churches, and festivals, not recognizing the guiding hand of God

into Bethany; and he lodged there. 18. Now in the morning as he returned into the city, he hungered. 19. And when he saw a fig tree in the way, he came to it, and found nothing thereon, but leaves only, and said unto it, Let no fruit grow on thee henceforward for ever. And presently the fig tree withered away.[8] 20. And when the disciples saw it, they marvelled, saying, How soon is the fig tree withered away! 21. Jesus answered and said unto them, Verily I say unto you, If ye have faith, and doubt not, ye shall not only do this which is done to the fig tree, but also if ye shall say unto this mountain, Be thou removed, and be thou cast into the sea; it shall be done. 22. And all things, whatsoever ye shall ask in prayer, believing, ye shall receive. 23. And when he was come into the temple, the chief priests and the elders of the people came unto him as he was teaching, and said, By what authority doest thou these things? and who gave thee this authority? 24. And Jesus answered and said unto them, I also will ask you one thing, which if ye tell me, I in like wise will tell you by what authority I do these things. 25. The baptism of John, whence was it? from heaven, or of men? And they reasoned with themselves, saying, If we shall say, From heaven; he will say unto us, Why did ye not then believe him? 26. But if we shall say, Of men; we fear the people;[9] for all hold John as a prophet. 27. And they answered Jesus, and said, We cannot tell. And he said unto them, Neither tell I you by what authority I do these things.[10] 28. But what think ye? A certain man had two

---

in everyday life, not to mention those who would even limit God to a physical form, such as a man.

[8] 19. *And presently the fig tree withered away.* It was too early in the season for figs (it was before Pesach, cf. Mark 11:13). It is also a violation of Torah (Deuteronomy 20:19) to destroy fruit trees, even those surrounding and enemy's city in time of war (cf. Asher Norman, *Twenty–Six Reasons Why Jews Don't Believe in Jesus,* Los Angeles: Black White and Read Publishing, 2007, 41).

[9] 26. *But if we shall say, Of men; we fear the people.* It is the mob rule that gives Jesus his "authority." (Cf. Matthew 21:46.)

[10] 27. *Neither tell I you by what authority I do these things.* Jesus does not show that he has any divine authority in disobeying the Torah (Deuteronomy 18:15–22). According to Matthew, his "authority" is that he is backed by an armed mob.

sons;[11] *and he came to the first, and said, Son, go work to day in my vineyard. 29. He answered and said, I will not: but afterward he repented, and went. 30. And he came to the second, and said likewise. And he answered and said, I go, sir: and went not. 31. Whether of them twain did the will of his father? They say unto him, The first. Jesus saith unto them, Verily I say unto you, That the publicans and the harlots go into the kingdom of God before you. 32. For John came unto you in the way of righteousness, and ye believed him not: but the publicans and the harlots believed him: and ye, when ye had seen it, repented not afterward, that ye might believe him. 33. Hear another parable:*[12] *There was a certain*

---

[11] 28. *A certain man had two sons.* This is one of the most confused and mangled parables in the New Testament. There are three different versions of it.

In the first version (supported by ℵ, C, K, W, Δ, Π, it[c, q], vg, syr[c, p, h]) it has the first son say, "No," but he afterwards repents. The second son says, "Yes," but he does nothing. When Jesus asks which did the will of the father, they say ὁ πρῶτος (the first).

In the second version (supported by D, it[pa, b, d, e, ff2, h, l], syr[s]), the first son says, "No," but he repents, and the second son says, "Yes," but he does nothing. When Jesus asks which did the will of the father, they say ὁ ἔσχατος (the latter).

In the third version, the first son says, "Yes," but he does nothing, and the second son says, "No," but he repents. B has ὁ ὕστερος (the last); Θ, f^{13}, 700, syr[pal] has ὁ ἔσχατος, (the latter). The modern Greek texts usually follow B (ὁ ὕστερος), but it is deliberately mistranslated as "the first."

"Because [the second version] is the most difficult of the three forms of text, several scholars (Lachmann, Mers, Wellhausen, Hirsch [not the famous rabbi]) have thought that it must be preferred as readily accounting for the rise of the other two as improvements of it. But [the second version] is not only difficult, it is nonsensical—the son who said 'Yes' but does nothing obeys his father's will! Jerome, who knew of manuscripts in his day that read the nonsensical answer, suggested that though perversity the Jews intentionally gave an absurd reply in order to spoil the point of the parable...because such explanations attribute to the Jews, or to Matthew, far-fetched psychological or overly-subtle literary motives, the Committee judged that the origin of reading [the second version] is due to copyists who either committed a transcriptional blunder or who were motivated by anti-Pharisaic bias." Metzger, *A Textual Commentary on the Greek New Testament*, p. 45.

[12] 33. *Hear another parable.* There is no more teaching of love and forgiveness. The parables Jesus speaks after he takes control of the temple are of murder and vengeance. Gone is the "meek and loving" Jesus; the Jesus who marched into Jerusalem with the large mob of followers from Jericho is a Jesus who is vindic-

householder, which planted a vineyard, and hedged it round about, and digged a winepress in it, and built a tower, and let it out to husbandmen, and went into a far country: 34. And when the time of the fruit drew near, he sent his servants to the husbandmen, that they might receive the fruits of it. 35. And the husbandmen took his servants, and beat one, and killed another, and stoned another. 36. Again, he sent other servants more than the first: and they did unto them likewise. 37. But last of all he sent unto them his son, saying, They will reverence my son. 38. But when the husbandmen saw the son, they said among themselves, This is the heir; come, let us kill him, and let us seize on his inheritance. 39. And they caught him, and cast him out of the vineyard, and slew him.[13] *40. When the lord therefore of the vineyard cometh, what will he do unto those husbandmen? 41. They say unto him, He will miserably destroy those wicked men, and will let out his vineyard unto other husbandmen, which shall render him the fruits in their seasons. 42. Jesus saith unto them, Did ye never read in the scriptures, The stone which the builders rejected,*[14] *the same is become the head of the corner: this is the Lord's doing, and it is marvellous in our eyes? 43. Therefore say I unto you, The kingdom of God shall be taken from you, and given to a nation bringing forth the fruits thereof.*[15]

---

tive and remorseless. As the day wears on, and his arguments with the Sadducees become more heated, he calls the Sadducees a "den of thieves," hypocrites. This finally leads to his outburst of condemnation in chapter 23.

[13] *39. And they caught him, and cast him out of the vineyard, and slew him.* Cf. Mark 12:8, where they kill him first, then cast him out of the vineyard. The Western texts also follow the sequence in Mark (D, Θ, it[a, b, c, d, e, ff2, h, rl]).

[14] *42. The stone which the builders rejected.* Cf. Psalm 118:22. "This verse refers to David, who was despised and rejected by his own father and brothers (*Targum*)." Radak also interprets the stone as Israel, the "cornerstone" of the world. *Artscroll Tehillim*, Rabbi Avrohom Chaim Feuer, Brooklyn: Mesorah Publications, 1995, 1411.

[15] *43. The kingdom of God shall be taken from you, and given to a nation bringing forth the fruits thereof.* This is the basis of the church's "replacement theology," or "supersessionism," wherein the church has replaced Israel as the "chosen people" and the inheritor of God's promises to Israel. This was a concept developed by the early church fathers based on New Testament texts like Matthew 21:43. This concept that God punishes and abandons Israel forever is

44. And whosoever shall fall on this stone shall be broken:[16] *but on whomsoever it shall fall, it will grind him to powder. 45. And when the chief priests and Pharisees had heard his parables, they perceived that he spake of them. 46. But when they sought to lay hands on him, they feared the multitude, because they took him for a prophet.*

---

totally alien to the *Tanach*.

[16] 44. *And whosoever shall fall on this stone shall be broken.* Not found in 𝔭[104], which is a very early text (mid-second century).

XXII

1. And Jesus answered and spake unto them again by parables, and said, 2. The kingdom of heaven is like unto a certain king,[1] which made a marriage for his son, 3. And sent forth his servants to call them that were bidden to the wedding: and they would not come. 4. Again, he sent forth other servants, saying, Tell them which are bidden, Behold, I have prepared my dinner: my oxen and my fatlings are killed, and all things are ready: come unto the marriage. 5. But they made light of it, and went their ways, one to his farm, another to his merchandise: 6. And the remnant took his servants, and entreated them spitefully, and slew them. 7. But when the king heard thereof, he was wroth: and he sent forth his armies, and destroyed those murderers, and burned up their city. 8. Then saith he to his servants, The wedding is ready, but they which were bidden were not worthy. 9. Go ye therefore into the highways, and as many as ye shall find, bid to the marriage. 10. So those servants went out into the highways, and gathered together all as many as they found, both bad and good: and the wedding was furnished with guests. 11. And when the king came in to see the guests, he saw there a man which had not on a wedding garment: 12. And he saith unto him, Friend, how camest thou in hither not having a wedding garment? And he was speechless. 13. Then said the king to the servants, Bind him hand and foot, and take him away, and cast him into outer darkness; there shall be weeping and gnashing

---

[1] *22:2. The kingdom of heaven is like unto a certain king.* The Parable of the Unfashionable Guest. As with many of Jesus's parables, they make little sense when read literally; only with a Gnostic interpretation would they have been understood by the early Gnostic Christians. Here we have a parable about a king who hosts a wedding for his son and twice sends his servants out to invite people to the wedding. The servants are ignored the first time, and the second time they are mocked and killed by some of the invited guests. The king responds by slaughtering the people who killed his servants and burning down the entire city. He then drags people off the street to be his "guests," regardless of whether or not they are dressed properly. One man, who is not dressed properly, is "bound hand and foot" and "cast into the outer darkness." This parable has an entirely different lesson from that of the lilies of the field in Matthew 6:28–31, where Jesus teaches us not to worry about what we are wearing. In the Parable of the Unfashionable Guest, we are supposed to worry about being well dressed.

of teeth. 14. For many are called, but few are chosen. 15. Then went the Pharisees, and took counsel how they might entangle him in his talk. 16. And they sent out unto him their disciples with the Herodians, saying, Master, we know that thou art true, and teachest the way of God in truth, neither carest thou for any man: for thou regardest not the person of men. 17. Tell us therefore, What thinkest thou? Is it lawful to give tribute unto Caesar, or not? 18. But Jesus perceived their wickedness, and said, Why tempt ye me, ye hypocrites? 19. Shew me the tribute money. And they brought unto him a penny. 20. And he saith unto them, Whose is this image and superscription? 21. They say unto him, Caesar's. Then saith he unto them, Render therefore unto Caesar the things which are Caesar's; and unto God the things that are God's. 22. When they had heard these words, they marvelled, and left him, and went their way. 23. The same day came to him the Sadducees, which say that there is no resurrection, and asked him, 24. Saying, Master, Moses said, If a man die, having no children, his brother shall marry his wife, and raise up seed unto his brother. 25. Now there were with us seven brethren: and the first, when he had married a wife, deceased, and, having no issue, left his wife unto his brother: 26. Likewise the second also, and the third, unto the seventh. 27. And last of all the woman died also. 28. Therefore in the resurrection whose wife shall she be of the seven? for they all had her. 29. Jesus answered and said unto them, Ye do err, not knowing the scriptures, nor the power of God. 30. For in the resurrection they neither marry, nor are given in marriage, but are as the angels of God in heaven.[2] 31. But as touching the resurrection of the dead, have ye not read that which was spoken unto you by God, saying, 32. I am the God of Abraham, and the God of Isaac, and the God of Jacob? God is not the God of the dead, but of the living. 33. And when the multitude heard this, they were astonished at his doctrine. 34. But when the Pharisees had heard that he had put the Sadducees to silence, they were gathered together. 35. Then one of them, which

---

[2] 30. *but are as the angels of God in heaven.* Vaticanus and other early manuscripts omit *of God.*

  Text: 𝕂, ℵ, W, f, it (some MSS.), vg, sy^p, bo
  Omit *of God*: B, D, Θ, λ, it (some MSS.), sy^c, sy^s, sa

was a lawyer, asked him a question, tempting him, and saying, 36. Master, which is the great commandment in the law? 37. Jesus said unto him, Thou shalt love the Lord thy God with all thy heart, and with all thy soul, and with all thy mind. 38. This is the first and great commandment. 39. And the second is like unto it, Thou shalt love thy neighbour as thyself. 40. On these two commandments hang all the law and the prophets. 41. While the Pharisees were gathered together, Jesus asked them, 42. Saying, What think ye of Christ? whose son is he? They say unto him, The Son of David. 43. He saith unto them, How then doth David in spirit call him Lord, saying, 44. The LORD said unto my Lord,[3] Sit thou on my right hand, till I make thine enemies thy footstool? 45. If David then call him Lord, how is he his son? 46. And no man was able to answer him a word, neither durst any man from that day forth ask him any more questions.

---

[3] 44. *The LORD said unto my lord.* The correct translation of Psalm 110:1 reads, *The Lord said to my master* (Hirsch). According to Rabbi Hirsch, this psalm is about David and focuses on two aspects of the king: his subduing of the pagan nations by the sword and his lofty spiritual mission, which was to turn the hearts of men to HaShem and his Torah (Hirsch, commentary to Ps. 110). Verse 6 of the psalm says, *He shall one day judge the cadaverous among the nations* (Hirsch), which is an allusion to the final victory of Israel over the gentiles who have built their kingdoms upon the victims of brutality and murder and created a "mighty land" whose riches stem from the corpses of the innocent.

XXIII

1. Then spake Jesus to the multitude, and to his disciples,[1] *2. Saying, The scribes and the Pharisees sit in Moses' seat: 3. All therefore whatsoever they bid you observe, that observe and do;*[2]

---

[1] 23:1. *Then spake Jesus to the multitude, and to his disciples.* The author of Matthew begins Jesus's public ministry with the Sermon on the Mount; he ends it (cf. Matt. 24:1, 3) with the Diatribe in the Temple. Chapter 23 is a long harangue against the Pharisees and, by association, the Jews. It is interesting to read the Sermon on the Mount alongside the Diatribe in the Temple, for they contradict each other in their tone toward both the teachers of Judaism and Judaism itself. This is arguably the most anti-Semitic chapter in the entire New Testament, and many of the great evils that Christians have afflicted upon the Jews—the crusades, the Inquisition, the pogroms, the Holocaust—have their roots here. The internal evidence is that this entire chapter is a fabrication [cf. note to v. 35, below] that was added some time in the second century when Matthew achieved its final form.

[2] 3. *Saying, The scribes and the Pharisees sit in Moses' seat ... All therefore whatsoever they bid you observe, that observe and do.* This is in accordance with Deuteronomy 17:9–12, where Moses taught, *You shall come to the Kohanim, the Levites, and to the judge who will be in those days; you shall inquire and they will tell you the word of judgment. You shall do according to the word that they will tell you, from that place that HASHEM will choose, and you shall be careful to do according to everything that they will teach you. According to the teaching that they will teach you and according to the judgment that they will say to you, shall you do; you shall not deviate from the word that they will tell you, right or left. And the man that will act with willfulness, not listening to the Kohen who stands there to serve HASHEM, your God, or to the judge, that man shall die, and you shall destroy the evil from among Israel.*

One of the great challenges of the Noahide movement is the full acceptance of the Oral Torah. Sadly, many Noahides (even many of the self-appointed leaders) do not view the Oral Law as being as authoritative as the Written Law; they still have the Christian view that the Talmud is simply a lot of "manmade" rules and regulations. Again, the view that the "scripture" (i.e., the Written Torah) has greater authority is a Christian attitude, not a Jewish one. Christianity is a purely mystical religion that focuses on spirituality and emotion. The Noahide Law is legalistic in nature, for the entire discourse in the Talmud, as expounded in *Sanhedrin* 56a–60a, is concerned with which of the 613 commandments of the Torah a non-Jew is culpable for in a *beis din*, or a Noahide court of law. A Noahide can be as "spiritual" or as "mystical" as he or she desires, but Noahides who complain about the Noahide Law being "legalistic" are not looking at the Torah from a rabbinic point of view. As Dayan Dr. I. Grunfeld as written, "When

but do not ye after their works: for they say, and do not. 4. For they bind heavy burdens and grievous to be borne,³ and lay them on men's shoulders; but they themselves will not move them with one of their fingers. 5. But all their works they do for to be seen of men:⁴ they make broad their phylacteries, and enlarge the borders of their garments, 6. And love the uppermost rooms at feasts, and the chief seats in the synagogues, 7. And greetings in the markets, and to be called of men, Rabbi, Rabbi. 8. But be not ye called Rabbi: for one is your Master, even Christ; and all ye are brethren. 9. And call no man your father⁵ upon the earth: for one is your Father, which is in heaven. 10. Neither be ye called masters: for one is your Master, even Christ. 11. But he that is greatest among you shall be your servant. 12. And whosoever shall exalt himself shall be abased; and he that shall humble himself shall be exalted. 13. But woe unto you, scribes and Pharisees, hypocrites! for ye shut up the kingdom of heaven against men:⁶ for ye neither go in

---

we speak of Revelation we mean both Written and Oral Law … [t]he doctrine of the Divine origin of both Written and Oral Law, their inseparable unity and their contemporaneous revelation, is part of the very fundamentals of Judaism" (Intro. to *Horeb,* New York: The Soncino Press, 1994, xlv). There is certainly a mystical and spiritual side to the Torah (consider the kabbalah), but the purpose of the study of Jewish mysticism is to glean a greater understanding of the mitzvot, not to supplant the legal dicta of the Oral Law.

³ 4. *For they bind heavy burdens and grievous to be borne.* Although this phrase is found in Vaticanus and other early texts, many other early manuscripts (including Sinaiticus) do not have *and grievous to be borne.* Codex Bezae reads *and not grievous to be borne.*
    Text: 𝕶, B, W, Θ, φ, it (some MSS.), vg, sa
    Omit *and grievous to be borne*: ℵ, λ, it (some MSS.), sy^c, sy^s, sy^p, bo
    Include *and not grievous to be borne*: D

⁴ 5. *But all their works they do for to be seen of men.* This goes against what Jesus taught earlier. Cf. Matthew 5:16, *Let your light so shine before men, that they may see your good works, and glorify your Father which is in heaven.*

⁵ 9. *And call no man your father.* Christians call their priests "Father So-and-so," and instead of rabbi, they use the titles like bishops, cardinals, and popes.

⁶ 13. *for ye shut up the kingdom of heaven against men.* Earlier, Jesus said that those who did not keep the Torah would be denied the World to Come. Cf. Matthew 7:22–23, *Many will say to me in that day, Lord, Lord, have we not proph-*

yourselves, neither suffer ye them that are entering to go in. 14. Woe unto you, scribes and Pharisees, hypocrites! for ye devour widows' houses, and for a pretense make long prayer: therefore ye shall receive the greater damnation.[7] *15. Woe unto you, scribes and Pharisees, hypocrites! for ye compass sea and land to make one proselyte, and when he is made, ye make him twofold more the child of hell than yourselves. 16. Woe unto you, ye blind guides, which say, Whosoever shall swear by the temple, it is nothing; but whosoever shall swear by the gold of the temple, he is a debtor! 17. Ye fools and blind: for whether is greater, the gold, or the temple that sanctifieth the gold? 18. And, Whosoever shall swear by the altar, it is nothing; but whosoever sweareth by the gift that is upon it, he is guilty. 19. Ye fools*[8] *and blind: for whether is greater, the gift, or the altar that sanctifieth the gift? 20. Whoso therefore shall swear by the altar, sweareth by it, and by all things thereon. 21. And whoso shall swear by the temple, sweareth by it, and by him that dwelleth therein. 22. And he that shall swear by heaven, sweareth by the throne of God, and by him that sitteth thereon. 23. Woe unto you, scribes and Pharisees, hypocrites! for ye pay tithe of mint and*

---

esied in thy name? and in thy name have cast out devils? and in thy name done many wonderful works? And then will I profess unto them, I never knew you: depart from me, ye that work against the Law.

[7] *14. Woe unto you, scribes and Pharisees, hypocrites! for ye devour widows' houses, and for a pretence make long prayer: therefore ye shall receive the greater damnation.* This textual corruption is often found after verse 12. It is absent from many of the early Greek witnesses, including Sinaiticus, Vaticanus, Bezae, and Origen.

    Text: (sometimes this verse is found after verse 12) = Mark 12:40; Luke 20:47: 𝕂, W, φ, it (some MSS.), vg (some MSS.), sy^c, sy^p

    Omit verse: ℵ, B, D, Θ, λ, it (some MSS.), vg (some MSS.), sy^s, sa, bo, Origen

[8] *19. Ye fools.* Cf. Matthew 5:22, where Jesus violates his own rule: *whosoever shall say, Thou fool, shall be in danger of hell fire.* "Jesus recognized two absolutely mortal sins. One was … unbrotherly arrogance, such as the arrogance of the intellectual toward the poor in spirit, when the intellectual hurls at his brother the exclamation 'Thou fool!'" (Max Weber, *Economy and Society*, Gunther Roth and Claus Wittich, eds., Berkeley: University of California Press, 1978, 632).

anise and cummin, and have omitted the weightier matters of the law, judgment, mercy, and faith:[9] *these ought ye to have done, and not to leave the other undone. 24. Ye blind guides, which strain at a gnat, and swallow a camel. 25. Woe unto you, scribes and Pharisees, hypocrites! for ye make clean the outside of the cup and of the platter, but within they are full of extortion and excess. 26. Thou blind Pharisee, cleanse first that which is within the cup and platter, that the outside of them may be clean also. 27. Woe unto you, scribes and Pharisees, hypocrites! for ye are like unto whited sepulchres, which indeed appear beautiful outward, but are within full of dead men's bones, and of all uncleanness. 28. Even so ye also outwardly appear righteous unto men, but within ye are full of hypocrisy and iniquity.*[10] *29. Woe unto you, scribes and Pharisees, hypocrites! because ye build the tombs of the prophets, and garnish the sepulchres of the righteous, 30. And say, If we had been in the days of our fathers, we would not have been partakers with them in the blood of the prophets. 31. Wherefore ye be witnesses unto yourselves, that ye are the children of them which killed the prophets. 32. Fill ye up then the measure of your fathers. 33. Ye serpents, ye generation of vipers, how can ye escape the damnation of hell? 34. Wherefore, behold, I send unto you prophets, and wise men, and scribes: and some of them ye shall kill and crucify; and some of them shall ye scourge in your synagogues, and persecute them from city to city: 35. That upon you may come all the righteous blood shed upon the earth, from the blood of righteous Abel unto the blood of Zacharias son of Barachias, whom ye slew between the temple and the altar.*[11] *36. Verily I say unto you, All these things*

---

[9] 23. *the weightier matters of the law, judgment, mercy, and faith.* In Matthew 7:1, Jesus tells his followers *judge not, that ye be not judged*, yet in this chapter he is judging the Pharisees without mercy.

[10] 28. *but within ye are full of hypocrisy and [lawlessness].* Cf. Matthew 5:29, *And if thy right eye offend thee, pluck it out, and cast it from thee: for it is profitable for thee that one of thy members should perish, and not that thy whole body should be cast into hell.* Deut. 14:1 says, *You are children to HaShem, your God—you shall not cut yourselves.*

[11] 35. *the blood of Zacharias son of Barachias, whom ye slew between the temple and the altar.* This is the verse that makes this chapter suspect. There were two prophets named Zechariah in the *Tanach*. One was the prophet who was

shall come upon this generation. 37. O Jerusalem, Jerusalem, thou that killest the prophets, and stonest them which are sent unto thee, how often would I have gathered thy children together, even as a hen gathereth her chickens under her wings, and ye would not! 38. Behold, your house is left unto you desolate.[12] *39. For I say unto you, Ye shall not see me henceforth, till ye shall say, Blessed is he that cometh in the name of the Lord.*

---

the son of Jehoiada (see 2 Chronicles 24:20–21) and was slain in the temple during the time of Joash son of Ahaziah, king of Judah when the First Temple stood. The other prophet, Zechariah son of Berechiah, was the author of one of the books in *Trei Asar*, the Twelve Prophets. The writings of Josephus, however, tell of a different Zechariah, one who was killed in the final years of the Roman occupation: "and as they intended to have Zacharias the son of Baruch, one of the most eminent of the citizens, slain ... so two of the boldest of them fell upon Zacharias in the middle of the temple, and slew him." (*War of the Jews*, Book iv, ch. vii, v. ii). The event recounted in Matthew 23:35 occurred nearly forty years after Jesus died.

[12] 38. *Behold, your house is left unto you desolate.* The word *desolate* is absent from Vaticanus and many other early manuscripts. Jesus's lament over Jerusalem in Matt. 23:37–39 is practically word for word the same in Luke 13:34–35. This is one of the famous "*Q*" passages, inserted into the text.

XXIV

1. And Jesus went out, and departed from the temple: and his disciples came to him for to shew him the buildings of the temple. 2. And Jesus said unto them, See ye not all these things? verily I say unto you, There shall not be left here one stone upon another, that shall not be thrown down.[1] *3. And as he sat upon the mount of Olives, the disciples came unto him privately, saying, Tell us, when shall these things be? and what shall be the sign of thy coming, and of the end of the world? 4. And Jesus answered and said unto them, Take heed that no man deceive you. 5. For many shall Come in my name, saying, I am Christ; and shall deceive many.*[2] *6. And ye shall hear of wars and rumours of wars: see that ye be*

---

[1] *24:2. And Jesus said unto them, See ye not all these things? verily I say unto you, There shall not be left here one stone upon another, that shall not be thrown down.* Josephus wrote about others who would deceive the people: "These works, that were done by the robbers, filled the city with all sorts of impiety. And now these impostors and deceivers persuaded the multitude to follow them into the wilderness, and pretended that they would exhibit manifest wonders and signs, that should be performed by the providence of God. And many that were prevailed on by them suffered the punishments of their folly; for Felix brought them back, and then punished them. Moreover, there came out of Egypt about this time to Jerusalem one that said he was a prophet, and advised the multitude of the common people to go along with him to the Mount of Olives, as it was called, which lay over against the city, and at the distance of five furlongs. He said further, that he would show them from hence how, at his command, the walls of Jerusalem would fall down; and he promised them that he would procure them an entrance into the city through those walls, when they were fallen down. Now when Felix was informed of these things, he ordered his soldiers to take their weapons, and came against them with a great number of horsemen and footmen from Jerusalem, and attacked the Egyptian and the people that were with him. He also slew four hundred of them, and took two hundred alive. But the Egyptian himself escaped out of the fight, but did not appear any more. And again the robbers stirred up the people to make war with the Romans, and said they ought not to obey them at all; and when any persons would not comply with them, they set fire to their villages, and plundered them" (*Antiquities of the Jews*, chapter 8:6).

[2] *5. For many shall come in my name, saying, I am Christ; and shall deceive many.* The *I am* here is ἐγώ εἰμι, the same Greek words Jesus uses in John 8:58. Many Christians have indeed come in the "name" of Jesus, saying that Jesus is the Christ, or Messiah. They have deceived many over the centuries.

not troubled: for all these things must come to pass, but the end is not yet. 7. For nation shall rise against nation, and kingdom against kingdom: and there shall be famines, and pestilences, and earthquakes, in divers places. 8. All these are the beginning of sorrows. 9. Then shall they deliver you up to be afflicted, and shall kill you: and ye shall be hated of all nations for my name's sake.[3] *10. And then shall many be offended, and shall betray one another, and shall hate one another. 11. And many false prophets shall rise, and shall deceive many. 12. And because iniquity shall abound, the love of many shall wax cold. 13. But he that shall endure unto the end, the same shall be saved. 14. And this gospel of the kingdom shall be preached in all the world for a witness unto all nations; and then shall the end come. 15. When ye therefore shall see the abomination of desolation,*[4] *spoken of by Daniel the prophet, stand in the holy place, (whoso readeth, let him understand:) 16. Then let them which be in Judaea flee into the mountains: 17. Let him which is on the housetop not come down to take any thing out of his house: 18. Neither let him which is in the field return back to take his clothes. 19. And woe unto them that are with child, and to them that give suck in those days! 20. But pray ye that your flight be not in the winter, neither on the sabbath day: 21. For then shall be great tribulation, such as was not since the beginning of the world to this time, no, nor ever shall be. 22. And except those days should be shortened, there should no flesh be saved: but for the elect's sake those days shall be shortened. 23. Then if any man shall say unto you, Lo, here is Christ, or there; believe it not. 24. For there shall arise false Christs, and false prophets, and shall shew great signs and wonders; insomuch that, if it were possible, they shall deceive the very elect. 25. Behold, I have told you before. 26. Wherefore if they shall say unto you, Behold, he is in the desert;*

---

[3] *9. Then shall they deliver you up to be afflicted, and shall kill you: and ye shall be hated of all nations for my name's sake.* Jews have been hated by Christians for being Christ-killers since the Middle Ages (or before).

[4] 15. *the abomination of desolation.* Cf. Daniel 11:31. According to *Malbim*, this refers to Hadrian, the Roman emperor who built a temple for idol worship on the site of the Holy Temple after the Bar Kochba revolt. This would date chapter 24 of the Gospel of Matthew no earlier than 135.

go not forth: behold, he is in the secret chambers; believe it not. 27. For as the lightning cometh out of the east, and shineth even unto the west; so shall also the coming of the Son of man be. 28. For wheresoever the carcase is, there will the eagles be gathered together. 29. Immediately after the tribulation of those days[5] shall the sun be darkened, and the moon shall not give her light, and the stars shall fall from heaven, and the powers of the heavens shall be shaken: 30. And then shall appear the sign of the Son of man in heaven: and then shall all the tribes of the earth mourn, and they shall see the Son of man coming in the clouds of heaven with power and great glory. 31. And he shall send his angels with a great sound of a trumpet, and they shall gather together his elect from the four winds, from one end of heaven to the other. 32. Now learn a parable of the fig tree; When his branch is yet tender, and putteth forth leaves, ye know that summer is nigh: 33. So likewise ye, when ye shall see all these things, know that it is near, even at the doors. 34. Verily I say unto you, This generation shall not pass, till all these things be fulfilled. 35. Heaven and earth shall pass away, but my words shall not pass away. 36. But of that day and hour knoweth no man, no, not the angels of heaven, but my Father only.[6] 37. But as the days of Noe were, so shall also the coming of the Son of man be. 38. For as in the days that were before the flood they were eating and drinking, marrying and giving in marriage, until the day that Noe entered into the ark, 39. And knew not until the flood came, and took them all away; so shall also the coming of the Son of man be. 40. Then shall two be in the field; the one

---

[5] 29. *Immediately after the tribulation of those days.* Cf. Isaiah 13:10. This was a prophecy concerning Babylon (Isaiah 13:1).

[6] 36. *But of that day and hour knoweth no man, no, not the angels of heaven, but my Father only.* The earliest Greek New Testament manuscripts, including Sinaiticus, Vaticanus, Bezae, and the early church father Irenaeus have *But about that day and hour no one knows, neither the angels of heaven, nor the Son, but only the Father*. The words *nor the Son* were removed in all later texts for obvious reasons.

>Omits: *nor the Son*: 𝕂, W, λ, vg, sy^s, sy^p, sa, bo, Didymus
>*But about that day and hour no one knows, neither the angels of heaven, nor the Son, but only the Father*: ℵ, B, D, Θ, φ, it, Irenaeus.

shall be taken, and the other left. 41. Two women shall be grinding at the mill; the one shall be taken, and the other left. 42. Watch therefore: for ye know not what hour your Lord doth come. 43. But know this, that if the goodman of the house had known in what watch the thief would come, he would have watched, and would not have suffered his house to be broken up. 44. Therefore be ye also ready: for in such an hour as ye think not the Son of man cometh. 45. Who then is a faithful and wise servant, whom his lord hath made ruler over his household, to give them meat in due season? 46. Blessed is that servant, whom his lord when he cometh shall find so doing. 47. Verily I say unto you, That he shall make him ruler over all his goods. 48. But and if that evil servant shall say in his heart, My lord delayeth his coming; 49. And shall begin to smite his fellowservants, and to eat and drink with the drunken; 50. The lord of that servant shall come in a day when he looketh not for him, and in an hour that he is not aware of, 51. And shall cut him asunder,[7] and appoint him his portion with the hypocrites: there shall be weeping and gnashing of teeth.

---

[7] 51. *And shall cut him asunder.* To put someone to death without a trial is a violation of the Torah (see Numbers 35:12).

XXV

1. Then shall the kingdom of heaven be likened unto ten virgins,[1] which took their lamps, and went forth to meet the bridegroom.[2] 2. And five of them were wise, and five were foolish. 3. They that were foolish took their lamps, and took no oil with them: 4. But the wise took oil in their vessels with their lamps. 5. While the bridegroom tarried, they all slumbered and slept. 6. And at midnight there was a cry made, Behold, the bridegroom cometh; go ye out to meet him. 7. Then all those virgins arose, and trimmed their lamps. 8. And the foolish said unto the wise, Give us of your oil; for our lamps are gone out. 9. But the wise answered, saying, Not so; lest there be not enough for us and you: but go ye rather to them that sell, and buy for yourselves. 10. And while they went to buy, the bridegroom came; and they that were ready went in with him to the marriage: and the door was shut. 11. Afterward came also the other virgins, saying, Lord, Lord, open to us. 12. But he answered and said, Verily I say unto you, I know you not. 13. Watch therefore, for ye know neither the day nor the hour wherein the Son of man cometh.[3] 14. For the kingdom of heaven is as a man travelling into a far country, who called his own servants, and delivered unto

---

[1] 25:1. *be likened unto ten virgins.* Chapter 25 starts out with two remarkable parables. The first is the Parable of the Pagan Wedding, where Jesus compares his "kingdom of heaven" to ten virgins who are getting ready to cavort with a bridegroom before and during his wedding. The question is this: why would Jesus use a pagan wedding complete with virgins (instead of a traditional Jewish wedding) as an example for teaching righteousness? In the Sermon on the Mount, he contrasted correct Torah-observant behavior with the pagan behavior of the gentiles, but here at the end of Matthew, he is cursing the teachers of the Torah (the Pharisees) and using pagan examples such as the parable of the pagan wedding. Was Jesus corrupted by pagan ideas, as the Talmud suggests? Or is this parable—indeed this chapter, if not this entire gospel—a second-century invention by Christian Gnostics?

[2] 1. *went forth to meet the bridegroom.* Many early texts, including Bezae and the Old Latin, include *and the bride.*

    Text: 𝕂, א, B, C, W, φ, sa, bo
    Add: *and the bride*: D, Θ, λ, it, vg, sy^s, sy^p

[3] 13. *wherein the Son of man cometh.* This part of the verse is not in many of the early Greek manuscripts.

them his goods. 15. And unto one he gave five talents, to another two, and to another one; to every man according to his several ability;[4] *and straightway took his journey. 16. Then he that had received the five talents went and traded with the same, and made them other five talents. 17. And likewise he that had received two, he also gained other two. 18. But he that had received one went and digged in the earth, and hid his lord's money. 19. After a long time the lord of those servants cometh, and reckoneth with them. 20. And so he that had received five talents came and brought other five talents, saying, Lord, thou deliveredst unto me five talents: behold, I have gained beside them five talents more. 21. His lord said unto him, Well done, thou good and faithful servant: thou hast been faithful over a few things, I will make thee ruler over many things: enter thou into the joy of thy lord. 22. He also that had received two talents came and said, Lord, thou deliveredst unto me two talents: behold, I have gained two other talents beside them. 23. His lord said unto him, Well done, good and faithful servant; thou hast been faithful over a few things, I will make thee ruler over many things: enter thou into the joy of thy lord. 24. Then he which had received the one talent came and said, Lord, I knew thee that thou art an hard man, reaping where thou hast not sown, and gathering where thou hast not strawed. 25. And I was afraid, and went and hid thy talent in the earth: lo, there thou hast that is thine. 26. His lord answered and said unto him, Thou wicked and slothful servant, thou knewest that I reap where I sowed not, and gather where I have not strawed:*[5] *27. Thou oughtest therefore to have put my money to the exchangers, and then at my coming I should have received mine own with usury. 28. Take therefore the talent*

---

[4] 15. *to every man according to his several ability.* Following the Parable of the Pagan Wedding comes the Parable of the Capitalists. In this parable, Jesus compares the "kingdom of heaven" to a capitalist who gives his three servants silver to invest for him while he is away. The two good capitalists invest it and have returns of 100 percent, which pleases the rich capitalist greatly. The third man, however, is a bad capitalist; he does not invest the money, but buries it in the ground, and thus does not get a return on his investment.

[5] 26. *thou knewest that I reap where I sowed not, and gather where I have not strawed.* The rich capitalist admits he is dishonest, but he still punishes the servant.

from him, and give it unto him which hath ten talents. 29. For unto every one that hath shall be given, and he shall have abundance:[6] *but from him that hath not shall be taken away even that which he hath. 30. And cast ye the unprofitable servant into outer darkness: there shall be weeping and gnashing of teeth. 31. When the Son of man shall come in his glory, and all the holy angels with him, then shall he sit upon the throne of his glory: 32. And before him shall be gathered all nations: and he shall separate them one from another, as a shepherd divideth his sheep from the goats: 33. And he shall set the sheep on his right hand, but the goats on the left. 34. Then shall the King say unto them on his right hand, Come, ye blessed of my Father, inherit the kingdom prepared for you from the foundation of the world: 35. For I was an hungred, and ye gave me meat: I was thirsty, and ye gave me drink: I was a stranger, and ye took me in: 36. Naked, and ye clothed me: I was sick, and ye visited me: I was in prison, and ye came unto me. 37. Then shall the righteous answer him, saying, Lord, when saw we thee and hungred, and fed thee? or thirsty, and gave thee drink? 38. When saw we thee a stranger, and took thee in? or naked, and clothed thee? 39. Or when saw we thee sick, or in prison, and came unto thee? 40. And the King shall answer and say unto them, Verily I say unto you, Inasmuch as ye have done it unto one of the least of these my brethren, ye have done it unto me.*[7] *41. Then shall he say also unto them on the left hand, Depart from me, ye cursed, into everlasting fire, prepared for the devil and his angels: 42. For I was an hungred, and ye gave me no meat: I was thirsty, and ye*

---

[6] 29. *For unto every one that hath shall be given, and he shall have abundance.* It is odd that this parable ends this way when it began with to every man according *to his several ability* (and "to each according to his need"?). The moral of this parable seems to be: capitalism is good, even if you acquire the investment capital through dishonest means. The Gnostic interpretation doubtless had a "spiritual" exegesis.

[7] 40. *And the King shall answer and say unto them, Verily I say unto you, Inasmuch as ye have done it unto one of the least of these my brethren, ye have done it unto me.* Both Clement of Alexandria (*Miscellanies* I.19:94, 5) and Tertullian (*On Prayer*, 26) add *you have seen your brother or sister; you have seen your God.* Cf. Matthew 12:50, where Jesus says that "his brethren" are those who do the "will of the Father," that is, those who keep the Torah.

gave me no drink: 43. I was a stranger, and ye took me not in: naked, and ye clothed me not: sick, and in prison, and ye visited me not. 44. Then shall they also answer him, saying, Lord, when saw we thee and hungred, or athirst, or a stranger, or naked, or sick, or in prison, and did not minister unto thee? 45. Then shall he answer them, saying, Verily I say unto you, Inasmuch as ye did it not to one of the least of these, ye did it not to me. 46. And these shall go away into everlasting punishment: but the righteous into life eternal.

XXVI

1. And it came to pass, when Jesus had finished all these sayings, he said unto his disciples, 2. Ye know that after two days is the feast of the passover, and the Son of man is betrayed to be crucified. 3. Then assembled together the chief priests, and the scribes, and the elders of the people, unto the palace of the high priest, who was called Caiaphas, 4. And consulted that they might take Jesus by subtilty, and kill him. 5. But they said, Not on the feast day, lest there be an uproar among the people. 6. Now when Jesus was in Bethany, in the house of Simon the leper,[1] 7. There came unto him a woman having an alabaster box of very precious ointment, and poured it on his head,[2] as he sat at meat. 8. But when his disciples saw it, they had indignation, saying, To what purpose is this waste? 9. For this ointment might have been sold for much, and given to the poor. 10. When Jesus understood it, he said unto them, Why trouble ye the woman? for she hath wrought a good work upon me. 11. For ye have the poor always with you; but me ye have not always. 12. For in that she hath poured this ointment on my body, she did it for my burial. 13. Verily I say unto you, Wheresoever this gospel shall be preached in the whole world, there shall also this, that this woman hath done, be told for a memorial of her. 14. Then one of the twelve, called Judas Iscariot, went unto the chief priests, 15. And said unto them, What will ye give me, and I will deliver him unto you? And they covenanted with him for thirty pieces of silver. 16. And from that time he sought opportunity to betray him. 17. Now the first day of the feast of unleavened bread the disciples came to Jesus, saying unto him, Where wilt thou that we prepare for thee to eat the passover? 18. And he said, Go into the city to

---

[1] 26:6. *Simon the leper.* An excellent place for a seditionist to hide out. No one would want to search the house of a leper.

[2] 7. *and poured it on his head.* "A king may be appointed only by a court of 70 elders, together with a prophet, as Joshua was appointed by Moses and his court, and as Saul and David, were appointed by Samuel of Ramah and his court" (*Rambam, Hilchot Melachim* 1:3). Unlike a true king of Israel, who was anointed in the manner described by *Rambam* (by a prophet and the Sanhedrin), Jesus was "anointed" by a prostitute in the house of a leper.

such a man, and say unto him, The Master saith, My time is at hand; I will keep the passover at thy house with my disciples. 19. And the disciples did as Jesus had appointed them; and they made ready the passover. 20. Now when the even was come, he sat down with the twelve. 21. And as they did eat, he said, Verily I say unto you, that one of you shall betray me. 22. And they were exceeding sorrowful, and began every one of them to say unto him, Lord, is it I? 23. And he answered and said, He that dippeth his hand with me in the dish, the same shall betray me. 24. The Son of man goeth as it is written of him: but woe unto that man by whom the Son of man is betrayed! it had been good for that man if he had not been born. 25. Then Judas, which betrayed him, answered and said, Master, is it I? He said unto him, Thou hast said. 26. And as they were eating, Jesus took bread, and blessed it, and brake it, and gave it to the disciples, and said, Take, eat; this is my body. 27. And he took the cup, and gave thanks, and gave it to them, saying, Drink ye all of it; 28. For this is my blood of the new testament,³ which is shed for many for the remission of sins. 29. But I say unto you, I will not drink henceforth of this fruit of the vine, until that day when I drink it new with you in my Father's kingdom. 30. And when they had sung an hymn, they went out into the mount of Olives. 31. Then

---

³ *28. For this is my blood of the new testament.* Another important alteration that affects Christian theology. The word *new* in the phrase *new testament* is not in any of the earliest manuscripts. It is absent in $\mathfrak{p}^{37}$, Sinaiticus, and Vaticanus. Also, none of the second-century church fathers use the word. Cf. Justin, *Apology* I.66:3: "For the apostles, in the writings which were composed by them, called gospels, have delivered what was demanded of them: that Jesus took bread, gave thanks, and said, '*Do this in remembrance of me; this is my body.*' And likewise taking the cup, and having given thanks, Jesus said, '*This is my blood.*' This was a theological teaching by later Christians to show that Jesus ushered in a "new" covenant with God. Moreover, drinking blood is strictly prohibited by the Torah for Jews — the Christian teaching of "transubstantiation"; that is, of wine becoming Jesus' blood, is a pagan teaching, and clearly a violation of God's Law. Also see Didache 9:1–5: "Concerning the Eucharist, celebrate it in this way: First, concerning the cup: 'We give thanks to you, our Father, for the Holy Vine of David your child, which you made known to us through Jesus your child; to you be glory forever.'"

Text: 𝐊, A, C, D, W, λ, φ, it, vg, sy^s, sy^p, sa, bo
Omit *new*: $\mathfrak{p}^{37}$, א, B, Θ

saith Jesus unto them, All ye shall be offended because of me this night: for it is written, I will smite the shepherd,[4] and the sheep of the flock shall be scattered abroad. 32. But after I am risen again, I will go before you into Galilee. 33. Peter answered and said unto him, Though all men shall be offended because of thee, yet will I never be offended. 34. Jesus said unto him, Verily I say unto thee, That this night, before the cock crow, thou shalt deny me thrice. 35. Peter said unto him, Though I should die with thee, yet will I not deny thee. Likewise also said all the disciples. 36. Then cometh Jesus with them unto a place called Gethsemane, and saith unto the disciples, Sit ye here, while I go and pray yonder. 37. And he took with him Peter and the two sons of Zebedee, and began to be sorrowful and very heavy.[5] 38. Then saith he unto them, My soul is exceeding sorrowful, even unto death: tarry ye here, and watch with me. 39. And he went a little further, and fell on his face, and prayed, saying, O my Father, if it be possible, let this cup pass from me:[6] nevertheless not as I will, but as thou wilt. 40. And he cometh unto the disciples, and findeth them asleep, and saith unto Peter, What, could ye not watch with me one hour? 41. Watch and pray, that ye enter not into temptation: the spirit indeed is willing, but the flesh is weak. 42. He went away again the second time, and prayed, saying, O my Father,[7] if this cup may not pass away from me, except I drink it, thy will be done. 43. And he came and found them asleep again: for their eyes were heavy. 44. And he left them, and went away again, and prayed the third time, saying the same

---

[4] 31. *I will smite the shepherd.* This is from Zechariah 13:7, which teaches about false prophets: *It will happen on that day, the prophets will be ashamed, each one of his vision when he prophesies it, and they will no longer wear the fur cloak in order to declare their lies. Rather, he will say, "I am not a prophet! I am a worker of the land, for a person took me as a herdsman since my youth"* (Zechariah 13:4–5). Cf. Matthew 3:4.

[5] 37. *and began to be sorrowful and very heavy.* His attempts to lead a rebellion having failed, Jesus becomes depressed.

[6] 39. *O my Father, if it be possible, let this cup pass from me.* Now Jesus begs for his life.

[7] 42. *and prayed, saying, O my Father.* If Jesus were God, why would he be praying to himself?

words. 45. Then cometh he to his disciples, and saith unto them, Sleep on now, and take your rest: behold, the hour is at hand, and the Son of man is betrayed into the hands of sinners. 46. Rise, let us be going: behold, he is at hand that doth betray me. 47. And while he yet spake, lo, Judas, one of the twelve, came, and with him a great multitude with swords and staves, from the chief priests and elders of the people. 48. Now he that betrayed him gave them a sign, saying, Whomsoever I shall kiss, that same is he: hold him fast. 49. And forthwith he came to Jesus, and said, Hail, master; and kissed him. 50. And Jesus said unto him, Friend, wherefore art thou come? Then came they, and laid hands on Jesus, and took him. 51. And, behold, one of them which were with Jesus stretched out his hand, and drew his sword, and struck a servant of the high priest's,[8] *and smote off his ear. 52. Then said Jesus unto him, Put up again thy sword into his place: for all they that take the sword*

---

[8] 51. *and drew his sword, and struck a servant of the high priest's.* In the Midrash *Sefer Otzar HaMidrashim* Vol. 2, p. 557, we read, "The original Christians, the Midrash says, were a violent group of political agitators. Far from being a pacifistic saint, the historical Yeshu was a political terrorist and a man of wanton violence. This side of him even comes through the white-washed version of him presented in the Christian Bible" (Rabbi Ariel Bar Tzadok).

This certainly makes the events in chapter 21 and following chapters clearer. Jesus comes into Jerusalem accompanied by a mob (or an army) that he assembled in Jericho. He deliberately attests to his messianic intention by riding on a donkey (and a colt, see Matthew 21:7), and then going straightway into the temple, not to offer sacrifices, but to take it over from the Sadducees (see Matthew 21:12). He refuses to tell the priests and elders what authority he has to do these things (see Matthew 21:27). He then teaches parables on two of his favorite subjects: revenge and killing (Matthew 21:33–44). The chief priests and the Pharisees, i.e., the Sadducee leaders, cannot remove him because of the mob he brought with him (see Matthew 21:46, 26:5). Chapters 22 to 25 show how Jesus continues his teaching of hatred toward the true teachers of the Torah (Matthew 23) and his themes of killing and revenge and destruction (cf. Mark 14:58, where Jesus teaches that he will destroy the temple and then rebuild it, obviously to "fulfill" another "prophecy"). When we strip the veneer of the "meek and loving" Jesus that Christianity teaches, we see a man entering Jerusalem with an armed mob (Matthew 26:51, Luke 22:49), taking over the temple, and teaching violence, hate, and destruction. What authority indeed did Jesus have to do these things? He even ignored his own teaching about the true leaders of Judaism: *The scribes and the Pharisees sit in Moses' seat: All therefore whatsoever they bid you observe, that observe and do* (Matthew 23:2–3).

shall perish with the sword.⁹ 53. Thinkest thou that I cannot now pray to my Father, and he shall presently give me more than twelve legions of angels? 54. But how then shall the scriptures be fulfilled, that thus it must be? 55. In that same hour said Jesus to the multitudes, Are ye come out as against a Thief with swords and staves for to take me? I sat daily with you teaching in the temple, and ye laid no hold on me.¹⁰ 56. But all this was done, that the scriptures of the prophets might be fulfilled.¹¹ Then all the disciples forsook him, and fled. 57. And they that had laid hold on Jesus led him away to Caiaphas the high priest,¹² where the scribes and the elders were assembled. 58. But Peter followed him afar off unto the high priest's palace, and went in, and sat with the servants, to see the end. 59. Now the chief priests, and elders, and all the council, sought false witness against Jesus, to put him to death; 60. But found none: yea, though many false witnesses came, yet found they none. At the last came two false witnesses, 61. And said, This fellow said, I am able to destroy the temple of God, and to build it in three days.¹³ 62. And the high priest arose, and said unto him, Answerest thou nothing? what is it which these witness against thee? 63. But Jesus held his peace. And the high priest answered and said unto him, I adjure thee by the living God, that thou tell us

---

⁹ 52. *for all they that take the sword shall perish with the sword.* Jesus sees that he and his disciples are outnumbered.

¹⁰ 55. *I sat daily with you teaching in the temple, and ye laid no hold on me.* It is explained earlier (Matthew 21:46) why they did not seize him (because of the mob Jesus brought with him from Jericho).

¹¹ 56. *But all this was done, that the scriptures of the prophets might be fulfilled.* The *Tanach* does not say that God will come to earth in human form, nor does it say that God will commit suicide to take away the sins of all mankind. Contrary to Christian teaching, nowhere in the *Tanach* is it even implied that the Torah is only temporary. Which scriptures, then, are to be fulfilled?

¹² 57. *Caiaphas the high priest.* We must remember that the priests were in control of the temple that Jesus and his legion of followers had taken over. To Caiaphas, Jesus was an insurrectionist.

¹³ 61. *This fellow said, I am able to destroy the temple of God, and to build it in three days.* John 2:19 has Jesus saying this very thing.

whether thou be the Christ, the Son of God.[14] 64. Jesus saith unto him, Thou hast said: nevertheless I say unto you, Hereafter shall ye see the Son of man sitting on the right hand of power, and coming in the clouds of heaven. 65. Then the high priest rent his clothes, saying, He hath spoken blasphemy; what further need have we of witnesses? behold, now ye have heard his blasphemy. 66. What think ye? They answered and said, He is guilty of death. 67. Then did they spit in his face, and buffeted him; and others smote him with the palms of their hands, 68. Saying, Prophesy unto us, thou Christ, Who is he that smote thee? 69. Now Peter sat without in the palace: and a damsel came unto him, saying, Thou also wast with Jesus of Galilee. 70. But he denied before them all, saying, I know not what thou sayest. 71. And when he was gone out into the porch, another maid saw him, and said unto them that were there, This fellow was also with Jesus of Nazareth. 72. And again he denied with an oath, I do not know the man. 73. And after a while came unto him they that stood by, and said to Peter, Surely thou also art one of them; for thy speech betrayeth thee. 74Then began he to curse and to swear, saying, I know not the man. And immediately the cock crew. 75And Peter remembered the word of Jesus, which said unto him, Before the cock crow, thou shalt deny me thrice. And he went out, and wept bitterly.

---

[14] 63. *I adjure thee by the living God, that thou tell us whether thou be the Christ, the Son of God.* This is not an official trial by the Sanhedrin, but by the Sadducees in the house of the high priest, who are asking Jesus if he is the Jewish Messiah. If Jesus answered yes, then he was then halachically bound to prove it, which he did not do.

XXVII

1. When the morning was come, all the chief priests and elders of the people took counsel against Jesus to put him to death: 2. And when they had bound him, they led him away, and delivered him to Pontius Pilate the governor. 3. Then Judas, which had betrayed him, when he saw that he was condemned, repented himself, and brought again the thirty pieces of silver to the chief priests and elders, 4. Saying, I have sinned in that I have betrayed the innocent blood. And they said, What is that to us? see thou to that. 5. And he cast down the pieces of silver in the temple, and departed, and went and hanged himself. 6. And the chief priests took the silver pieces, and said, It is not lawful for to put them into the treasury, because it is the price of blood. 7. And they took counsel, and bought with them the potter's field, to bury strangers in. 8. Wherefore that field was called, The field of blood, unto this day. 9. Then was fulfilled that which was spoken by Jeremy the prophet,[1] saying, And they took the thirty pieces of silver, the price of him that was valued, whom they of the children of Israel did value; 10. And gave them for the potter's field, as the Lord appointed me. 11. And Jesus stood before the governor: and the governor asked him, saying, Art thou the King of the Jews? And Jesus said unto him, Thou sayest. 12. And when he was accused of the chief priests and elders, he answered nothing. 13. Then said Pilate unto him, Hearest thou not how many things they witness against thee? 14. And he answered him to never a word; insomuch that the governor marvelled greatly. 15. Now at that feast the governor was wont to release unto the people a prisoner,[2] whom they would. 16. And they had

---

[1] *27:9. Then was fulfilled that which was spoken by Jeremy the prophet.* Verses 9 and 10 contain another "prophesy" that is not in the Tanach. It is a splicing of Zecheriah 11:12–13 and Jeremiah 19:1–13 and 32:6–9. Even a casual reading shows these verses have nothing to do with either Judas or Jesus.

[2] 15. *Now at that feast the governor was wont to release unto the people a prisoner.* No historical record of this doubtful custom exists.

then a notable prisoner,[3] *called Barabbas.*[4] *17. Therefore when they were gathered together, Pilate said unto them, Whom will ye that I release unto you? Barabbas, or Jesus which is called Christ? 18. For he knew that for envy they had delivered him. 19. When he was set down on the judgment seat, his wife sent unto him, saying, Have thou nothing to do with that just man: for I have suffered many things this day in a dream because of him. 20. But the chief priests and elders persuaded the multitude that they should ask Barabbas, and destroy Jesus. 21. The governor answered and said unto them, Whether of the twain will ye that I release unto you? They said, Barabbas. 22. Pilate saith unto them, What shall I do then with Jesus which is called Christ? They all say unto him, Let him be crucified. 23. And the governor said, Why, what evil hath he done? But they cried out the more, saying, Let him be crucified. 24. When Pilate saw that he could prevail nothing, but that rather a tumult was made, he took water, and washed his hands before the multitude, saying, I am innocent of the blood of this just person:*[5] *see ye to it. 25. Then answered all the people, and said, His blood be on us, and on our children.*[6] *26. Then released he Barabbas*

---

[3] 16. *a notable prisoner.* Cf. Mark 15:7 and Luke 23:19, which tell us that Barabbas was "an insurrectionist" and a "murderer." If Barabbas had committed insurrection, it would of course have been against the Romans. To put this in perspective, in the late eighteenth century, there was a band of insurrectionists and murderers who committed treason against England. Who were these evil insurrectionists? George Washington, John Adams, Thomas Jefferson, et al. To the Jews, Barabbas was a hero, not a criminal.

[4] 16. *called Barabbas.* Both Origen and some early manuscripts have his name as "Jesus Barabbas," or, "Jesus son of the Father," implying "Jesus, son of God."

    Text: 𝕶, ℵ, A, B, D, W, φ, it, vg, sy^p, sa, bo
    called *Jesus Barabbas*: Θ, λ, sy^s, Origen

[5] 24. *I am innocent of the blood of this just person.* Vaticanus, Bezae, and other early manuscripts omit the word *just.*

    Text: 𝕶, ℵ, A, W, λ, φ, it (some MSS.), vg, sy^p, bo
    Omit *just*: B, D, Θ, it (some MSS.), sy^s, sa

[6] 25. *Then answered all the people, and said, His blood be on us, and on our children.* This verse has been used for centuries as a justification for murdering Jews. In John 19:15, these same people say, *We have no king but Caesar,* which shows us where their sympathies lay; they were assimilationist Jews who were

unto them: and when he had scourged Jesus, he delivered him to be crucified. 27. Then the soldiers of the governor took Jesus into the common hall, and gathered unto him the whole band of soldiers. 28. And they stripped him, and put on him a scarlet robe. 29. And when they had platted a crown of thorns, they put it upon his head, and a reed in his right hand: and they bowed the knee before him, and mocked him, saying, Hail, King of the Jews! 30. And they spit upon him, and took the reed, and smote him on the head. 31. And after that they had mocked him, they took the robe off from him, and put his own raiment on him, and led him away to crucify him. 32. And as they came out, they found a man of Cyrene, Simon by name: him they compelled to bear his cross. 33. And when they were come unto a place called Golgotha, that is to say, a place of a skull, 34. They gave him vinegar to drink mingled with gall: and when he had tasted thereof, he would not drink. 35. And they crucified him, and parted his garments, casting lots: that it might be fulfilled which was spoken by the prophet, They parted my garments among them, and upon my vesture did they cast lots.[7] 36. And sitting down they watched him there; 37. And set up over his head his accusation[8] written, THIS IS JESUS THE KING OF THE JEWS. 38. Then were there two thieves crucified with him, one on the right hand, and another on the left. 39. And they that passed by reviled him, wagging their heads, 40. And saying, Thou that destroyest the temple, and buildest it in three days, save thyself. If thou be the Son of God, come down from the cross. 41.

---

allied with the Romans. Many righteous Jews were executed by the Romans simply because they refused to say these very words.

[7] 35. *that it might be fulfilled which was spoken by the prophet, They parted my garments among them, and upon my vesture did they cast lots.* To deal with the problem of Jesus not being mentioned anywhere in the Hebrew *Tanach*, Christians claim (through Gnostic interpretations) that Jesus "fulfilled" many of the prophecies of the Old Testament, such as the prophecy of Matthew 27:35. The problem with this "prophecy," like so many others, is that it was added to the text many centuries later. It is absent from all the early texts: א, A, B, D, L, W, Γ, Π, 33, 71, 157, 565, 700, 872c, it$^{ff2, 1}$, vg^{mss}, syr$^{p, s, hmg, pal}$, eth, pers^{p}.

[8] 37. *And set up over his head his accusation.* This shows that Jesus was indeed charged with sedition, for the charge is written there: *This is Jesus the King of the Jews.* This is an accusation of sedition, not blasphemy.

Likewise also the chief priests mocking him, with the scribes and elders, said, 42. He saved others; himself he cannot save. If he be the King of Israel, let him now come down from the cross, and we will believe him. 43. He trusted in God; let him deliver him now, if he will have him: for he said, I am the Son of God. 44. The thieves also, which were crucified with him, cast the same in his teeth.[9] 45. Now from the sixth hour there was darkness over all the land unto the ninth hour. 46. And about the ninth hour Jesus cried with a loud voice, saying, Eli, Eli, lama sabachthani?[10] that is to say, My God, my God, why hast thou forsaken me? 47. Some of them that stood there, when they heard that, said, This man calleth for Elias. 48. And straightway one of them ran, and took a spunge, and filled it with vinegar, and put it on a reed, and gave him to drink. 49. The rest said, Let be, let us see whether Elias will come to save him.[11] 50. Jesus, when he had cried again with a loud voice, yielded up the ghost. 51. And, behold, the veil of the temple was rent in twain[12] from the top to the bottom; and the earth did quake, and the rocks rent; 52. And the graves were opened; and many bodies of the saints which slept arose, 53. And came out of the graves after his

---

[9] 44. *The thieves also, which were crucified with him, cast the same in his teeth.* Both Matthew and Mark describe these two as "robbers" (Matthew 27:38, Mark 15:37), Luke describes them as "malefactors" or "criminals" (Luke 23:32), and John simply says they were "two others" (John 19:18). These two men were likely involved in Jesus's failed insurrection and were blaming him for its failure.

[10] 46. *Eli, Eli, lama sabachthani?* In a few manuscripts (א, B, 33, cop^{sa}, ^{bo}) the usual ἠλι (*my God*) is spelled ελωι, which is from the Aramaic rather than the Hebrew ἠλι. The word *lama* ("why") has a similar treatment, with both Hebrew and Aramaic spellings; λεμα (א, B, 33, 700, 998), which is from the Aramaic, and *lama* (D, Θ, 1, 22, 565, 1582), which is from the Hebrew. Likewise, Bezae (D) has the Hebrew term ζαφθανει.

[11] 49. *let us see whether Elias will come to save him.* The addition to this verse in Sinaiticus, Vaticanus, and a few other early texts of the words *And another took a spear and pierced his side, and out came water and blood* is doubtless an addition from John 19:34.

[12] 51. *And, behold, the veil of the temple was rent in twain.* Verses 51 to 53 tell of earthquakes and people popping out of graves and running around. One might think that such momentous events would have been recorded in other historical records.

resurrection, and went into the holy city, and appeared unto many. 54. Now when the centurion, and they that were with him, watching Jesus, saw the earthquake, and those things that were done, they feared greatly, saying, Truly this was the Son of God. 55. And many women were there beholding afar off, which followed Jesus from Galilee, ministering unto him: 56. Among which was Mary Magdalene, and Mary the mother of James and Joses, and the mother of Zebedee's children. 57 .When the even was come, there came a rich man of Arimathaea, named Joseph, who also himself was Jesus' disciple: 58. He went to Pilate, and begged the body of Jesus. Then Pilate commanded the body to be delivered. 59. And when Joseph had taken the body, he wrapped it in a clean linen cloth, 60. And laid it in his own new tomb, which he had hewn out in the rock: and he rolled a great stone to the door of the sepulchre, and departed. 61. And there was Mary Magdalene, and the other Mary, sitting over against the sepulchre. 62. Now the next day, that followed the day of the preparation, the chief priests and Pharisees came together unto Pilate, 63. Saying, Sir, we remember that that deceiver said, while he was yet alive, After three days I will rise again. 64. Command therefore that the sepulchre be made sure until the third day, lest his disciples come by night, and steal him away, and say unto the people, He is risen from the dead: so the last error shall be worse than the first. 65. Pilate said unto them, Ye have a watch: go your way, make it as sure as ye can. 66. So they went, and made the sepulchre sure, sealing the stone, and setting a watch.

XXVIII

1. In the end of the sabbath, as it began to dawn toward the first day of the week,[1] *came Mary Magdalene and the other Mary to see the sepulchre. 2. And, behold, there was a great earthquake: for the angel of the Lord descended from heaven, and came and rolled back the stone from the door, and sat upon it. 3. His countenance was like lightning, and his raiment white as snow: 4. And for fear of him the keepers did shake, and became as dead men. 5. And the angel answered and said unto the women, Fear not ye: for I know that ye seek Jesus, which was crucified. 6. He is not here: for he is risen, as he said. Come, see the place where the Lord lay.*[2] *7. And go quickly, and tell his disciples that he is risen from the dead; and, behold, he goeth before you into Galilee; there shall ye see him: lo, I have told you. 8. And they departed quickly from the sepulchre with fear and great joy; and did run to bring his disciples word. 9. And as they went to tell his disciples, behold, Jesus met them, saying, All hail. And they came and held him by the feet, and worshipped him. 10. Then said Jesus unto them, Be not afraid: go tell my brethren that they go into Galilee, and there shall they see me. 11. Now when they were going, behold, some of the watch came into the city, and shewed unto the chief priests all the things that were done. 12. And when they were assembled with the elders, and had taken counsel, they gave large money unto the soldiers, 13. Saying, Say ye, His disciples came by night, and stole him away while we slept. 14. And if this come to the governor's ears, we will persuade him, and secure you. 15. So they took the money, and did*

---

[1] 28:1. *it began to dawn toward the first day of the week.* The Greek text, Οψέ δέ σαββάτων, τῇ ἐπιφωσκούσῃ εἰς μίαν σαββάτων, is a phrase that means "as the first day began," that is, after sundown. Jesus did not arise on our Sunday, but on our Saturday night. Thus, Jesus could have only been dead for thirty hours or so, hardly the "three days and three nights" he had prophesied before (see Matt. 12:40).

[2] 6. *see the place where the lord lay.* Sinaiticus, Vaticanus, and a few other Greek manuscripts have *see the place where he lay.*

    see the place where the Lord lay: ℵ, A, C, D, W, λ, φ, it, vg, sy^{pl}

    see the place where he lay: ℵ, B, Θ, sy^s, sa, bo

as they were taught: and this saying is commonly reported among the Jews until this day. 16. Then the eleven disciples went away into Galilee, into a mountain where Jesus had appointed them. 17. And when they saw him, they worshipped him: but some doubted. 18. And Jesus came and spake unto them, saying, All power is given unto me in heaven and in earth. 19. Go ye therefore, and teach all nations, baptizing them in the name of the Father,[3] and of the Son, and of the Holy Ghost: 20. Teaching them to observe all things whatsoever I have commanded you:[4] and, lo, I am with you always,

---

[3] 19. *Go ye therefore, and teach all nations, baptizing them in the name of the Father.* Obviously, to convert them to Judaism. The Greek εἰς τὸ "into the Name," in Hebrew would be *HaShem*. Cf. Acts 8:16, 19:5, Romans 6:3, 1 Corinthians 1:13, 10:2, and Galatians 3:27.

[4] 20. *Teaching them to observe all things whatsoever I have commanded you.* Here at the end of the Gospel according to Matthew, we must ask ourselves a significant question: what did Jesus teach, the Torah or Gnostic "mysteries"? Many of the Gnostic writings from around the same time as the traditional gospels had a tremendous impact on the developing theology of the second century. Many had teachings that went against the teachings of Judaism. For instance, the epistle of Barnabas, a letter written in the second century, was read extensively in the early churches. The influence and popularity of this epistle was so great that it is found in the Codex Sinaiticus, which means that even by the mid-fourth century, it was considered canonical. In Barnabas 8:6 we read, *But as for that circumcision, in which the Jews trust, it is abolished.* In Barnabas 2:7–8: *Bring no more vain oblations, incense is an abomination unto me; your new moons and sabbaths; the calling of assemblies I cannot away with, it is iniquity, even the solemn meeting; your new moons and your appointed feasts my soul hateth. These things therefore hath God abolished, that the new law of our lord Jesus Christ, which is without the yoke of any such necessity, might have the spiritual offering of men themselves.* Barnabas 3:16: *Consider this also: although you have seen so great signs and wonders done among the people of the Jews, yet this notwithstanding the Lord hath forsaken them.* (*Lost Books of the Bible,* New York: Bell Publishing Co., 1979, 146). The epistle of Barnabas was considered genuine by the early church fathers Clement of Alexandria and Origen.

Another popular early epistle was supposedly written by no less than Jesus himself in answer to a letter from Abgarus, King of Edessa. This epistle was considered genuine by Eusebius [*Church History*, Book 1, chapter 13]:

     Chapter 1, Abgarus's letter:

1. Abgarus, king of Edessa, to Jesus the good Saviour, who appears at Jerusalem, greeting. 2. I have been informed concerting you and your cures, which are performed without the use of medicines and herbs. 3. For it is reported, that you cause the blind to see, the lame to walk, do both cleanse lepers, and cast out

even unto the end of the world. Amen.[5]

---

unclean spirits and devils, and restore them to health who have been diseased, and raisest up the dead; 4. All which when I heard, I was persuaded of one of these two, viz.: either that you are God himself descended from heaven, who do these things, or the son of God. 5. On this account therefore I have wrote to you, earnestly to desire you would take the trouble of a journey hither, and cure a disease which I am under. 6. For I hear the Jews ridicule you, and intend you mischief. 7. My city is indeed small, but neat, and large enough for us both.
 Chapter 2, Jesus's reply:
1. Abgarus, you are happy, forasmuch as you have believed on me, whom ye have not seen. 2. For it is written concerning me, that those who have seen me should not believe on me, that they who have not seen might believe and live. 3. As to that part of your letter, which relates to my giving you a visit, I must inform you that I must fulfill all the ends of my mission in this country, and after that be received up again to him who sent me. 4. But after my ascension I will send one of my disciples, who will cure your disease, and give life to you, and all that are with you [(*Lost Books of the Bible,* New York: Bell Publishing Co., 1979, 62–63).

Many of these books and writings were supported and validated by important early church fathers, including Clement of Alexandria (*Stromata* 1:21, 2:6–7), Irenaeus (*Contra Heres.* iv. 20:2), Origen (*Cont. Cels* 1:63), Eusebius (*History of the Church*, Book I, ch. 13:6–9), and Jerome. They thus influenced Christian theology. Yet there are also many Gnostic teachings in the canonical gospels as well, detailed and voluminous commentaries now lost. These writings, surviving and lost, lead us to the conclusion that either Jesus taught Gnosticism or these passages were inventions of the Hellenized Christians and inserted later into the text. Neither one of these conclusions is conducive to Christianity being a "divinely inspired" religion, for this means that Jesus either taught pagan mysticism or the Greek text of Matthew was heavily corrupted by later Christian scribes.

[5] 20. *Amen.* ἀμὴν is not found in any of the early Alexandrian or Western texts. It is somehow fitting that the final word of Matthew, the Hebrew word which signifies "truth" (cf. note on Matt. 5:18, above), is missing from the earliest manuscripts.

Shabbat 54b states: Anyone who has the power to admonish the people of his household and fails to do so is held responsible for their behavior. [If he can admonish] the inhabitants of his city, he is held responsible for their behavior. If he has the power to admonish the entire world, he is held responsible for them.[1]
—Rambam

---

[1] Maimonides, *Mishna Torah: Hilchos Teshuvah,* New York: Maznaim Publishing Corporation, 1987, 95.

Notes

Notes

Notes

Notes

Notes

Notes